DREAMS
of
REALITY

DREAMS
of
REALITY

by

Dr. John J. Petrovic

iUniverse, Inc.
Bloomington

DREAMS OF REALITY

iUniverse books may be ordered through booksellers or by contacting:

iUniverse
1663 Liberty Drive
Bloomington, IN 47403
www.iuniverse.com
1-800-Authors (1-800-288-4677)

Because of the dynamic nature of the Internet, any web addresses or links contained in this book may have changed since publication and may no longer be valid. The views expressed in this work are solely those of the author and do not necessarily reflect the views of the publisher, and the publisher hereby disclaims any responsibility for them.

Any people depicted in stock imagery provided by Thinkstock are models, and such images are being used for illustrative purposes only.
Certain stock imagery © Thinkstock.

ISBN: 978-1-4697-5153-5 (sc)
ISBN: 978-1-4697-5154-2 (ebk)

Printed in the United States of America

iUniverse rev. date: 01/30/2012

Dedication

This book is dedicated to those who seek to understand the reality of their existence.

Acknowledgements

The author expresses his heartfelt gratitude to his wife Blanche and their daughter for constant love and support throughout the dream of this lifetime. They share his dream and without them his reality would be so much less.

Table of Contents

But a Dream

He found himself walking down a line of railroad tracks that disappeared off into the distance. The sun was bright in the sky and the tracks were flanked by dense forest on either side, in places almost forming a canopy. It brought back a memory from his youth of a set of railroad tracks that had run close to a baseball field where he and his brother used to play. There was a sense of serenity and peace and silence; he felt alone in the world yet happy to be living the moment.

As he walked down the tracks in the warm sunshine, a slight breeze stirred the trees with a rustling sound. It was warm, but not too warm, a perfect day for walking with just his thoughts as companions. The tracks ran straight through the forest until they curved away at least a mile distant.

His senses seemed heightened as he walked along; the sunlight shone bright and clear and the surrounding forest was lush and green. He heard the gentle rustling sound of the trees and the sigh of the wind; into his nostrils floated the delicate smell of dense vegetation. With each step, his feet crunched the rocks that lay between the railroad ties and he felt the unevenness in his steps. The rails looked like liquid metal under the bright sun.

There was no one there but himself, he was alone with his thoughts. Where do these tracks go, he thought. They must lead to something otherwise why would a train be going there. It was quiet, so quiet as he walked along. There was no evidence of a train at either end of the tracks that he could see. He heard no train whistles or any noises of a train in motion.

Eventually, he came to the curve in the tracks and could see what was ahead. There was a large train trestle that spanned a deep gorge. At the other end of the trestle, the tracks curved away again out of his view. The gorge was spectacular and deep. It looked like it had a height of about 200 feet at its middle, and at the bottom was the rushing rapids of a river. The scene was beautiful and reminded him of an automobile trip he had made on the coast highway in California. The trestle was like a bridge over a gorge that he had driven across many years ago on vacation.

As he approached the entrance of the trestle, he saw that there was no walkway along the side of the tracks, just the tracks themselves. The trestle was a long one and looked to be about one hundred yards from beginning to end. Not much room for error if he was on the trestle and a train came along, he thought.

There was no indication of any train, so he began walking across. But when he reached the halfway point, to his horror he heard the shrill sound of a train whistle. A moment later, a train rounded the bend ahead of him and came charging over the trestle. It was too far to run back. He froze like a deer in the headlights. The train was coming fast, coming . . . . .

And then he woke up.

To his very great relief, he was lying in his bed and still very much alive. He felt drained. How real his dream had been at the time! It seemed like reality but was merely an illusion taking place in his mind.

But the real question is: Was he still in a different dream when he woke up? How would he know that the waking state he was now experiencing was his true reality?

That's an interesting question indeed, and one that was explored to some extent in the hit movie "The Matrix". I'm sure many of you have seen and been influenced by this movie. I must say that, for me, watching "The Matrix" was not only entertaining but also very thought-provoking.

Let me remind you of the story line. Computer programmer Thomas Anderson works in his corporate cubicle during the day, but at night he becomes Neo, an expert computer hacker. During his hacking activities, he has been receiving vague computer messages about "The Matrix" and he wants to know more.

After a rather traumatic series of events involving sinister agents, particularly an Agent Smith (who refers to him very formally as Mister Anderson), Neo makes contact with the mysterious Morpheus, who offers to reveal to him the secret of the Matrix if he will only agree to take a pill. Morpheus gives Neo a choice. Take the blue pill and all will be as before in his life. But take the red pill and Neo will discover the truth of the Matrix. Naturally, Neo chooses the red pill.

In actuality, the red pill is a computer program that disconnects Neo from the Matrix. He wakes up in his true body, which is floating in liquid in a processing pod and is connected to various nutrient tubes, and with an electrical connection linked directly into his brain. There are thousands and thousands of other pods stored there. The reality is that intelligent machines have battled humanity in the past, and when humans tried to cut off their solar energy supply by globally blocking out the sun, the machines turned the human species into bio-batteries. Since the machines apparently had a sense of morality, they provided a pseudo-reality to the human race in the form of the Matrix, which is a virtual reality. In the Matrix, humanity believes that it is the world of the year 1999, while it is actually the world of approximately 2199.

Once the machine stewards realize that Neo has become aware, they abruptly disconnect him from his pod bio-support and dump his body into a liquid waste tank to perish. But fortunately, he is rescued by Morpheus and taken aboard the ship Nebuchadnezzar, where he is physically nursed back to health by the crew. Morpheus and the crew are members of the human resistance against the machines. This resistance has been built up over time, and has a subterranean base of operations called Zion. They have developed technologies to fight the machines, as well as the ability to infiltrate and operate in the virtual reality of the Matrix in order to liberate more humans.

Neo is shocked by the austerity and strangeness of his new reality. He finds it difficult to accept until Morpheus plugs Neo's brain into the virtual reality and shows him the truth. Morpheus believes that Neo may the "The One", a human who has been prophesized to be the savior of the human race in their war with the machines. He begins training Neo in the advanced skills of the Matrix virtual reality. In the Matrix, the laws of physics can be bent so that superhuman feats become possible. Neo learns these skills extremely well. He is also told that injuries suffered in the Matrix can affect his body in the real world. If, for example, he is shot in the heart in the Matrix simulation, he will die in the real world. Neo thus realizes the dangers one can face in the Matrix, even though it is a virtual reality.

Morpheus takes Neo into the Matrix to visit the Oracle, along with a few others from the crew, among them Trinity a female crew member who feels a special closeness to Neo. The Oracle, a woman, is not a real person but rather a computer program that has been inserted into the Matrix by its originators for an unclear purpose. However, the Oracle is the source of the prophesy of "The One", and Morpheus wants Neo to meet the Oracle to confirm that he is indeed "The One". But the Oracle tells Neo that, while he has great powers to manipulate the Matrix, he is still lacking something. Neo takes this to mean that he is not "The One". However, discussions with the Oracle are not to be revealed to others, and so Morpheus still believes Neo to be "The One".

After visiting the Oracle, the group attempts to exit the Matrix via a hacked telephone line, but is ambushed by Matrix Agents because one of the crew members who has remained aboard the Nebuchadnezzar has become a traitor, making a deal with the Agents to give up Morpheus if he is allowed to live like a king in the Matrix (he can no longer tolerate the austerity of the real world). This crew member is killed, but not before he kills a number of the other crew members. Also, Morpheus is captured by the Agents, essentially sacrificing himself so that Neo, who he believes to be "The One", can make it back to the ship.

The Agents take Morpheus to a building, where they attempt to extract from him the location of Zion, the subterranean headquarters of the resistance in the real world. Meanwhile, Neo and Trinity reenter the Matrix to rescue Morpheus. They manage to do so and Trinity and Morpheus transport themselves back to the ship. But Agents intercept Neo before he can transport back and he must flee from them to another Matrix location where he can get back to the real world. In the meantime, "sentinel" killing machines have converged on the Nebuchadnezzar in the real world and are threatening to destroy it. Before Neo can transport himself back though, he is confronted by his nemesis Agent Smith, who shoots him through the heart, killing him in the Matrix and thus in reality in his real body onboard the ship.

But Trinity cannot accept Neo's death and whispers to his body that the Oracle had told she would fall in love with "The One". She refuses to accept his death and kisses him, whereupon Neo comes back from the dead in both the Matrix and the real world. The Agents shoot volleys of bullets at him, but he simply raises his palm and stops their bullets in mid-air because he now has complete control of the Matrix—he can see the content of its underlying computer code. Agent Smith makes a final attempt to kill him, but his punches are effortlessly blocked, and Neo destroys him. The other Agents flee, and Neo returns to the real world in time for the ship's electromagnetic pulse weapon to destroy the sentinels that had already breached the craft's hull.

The movie ends with Neo returning to the Matrix and promising that he will free the humans from their bondage. It seems that he actually is "The One". He now has a full set of Matrix superhuman powers, and in the final scene he flies through the air, just like Superman.

Yes, the Matrix was a wonderful movie. For those living in the Matrix, life was indeed just a dream. So how do we know that we are not doing the same? The nature of our reality is what we will be exploring in this book.

Reality of a Lifetime

The realities of a person's lifetime are conception/gestation, birth, infancy, childhood, teenager, young adult, adult, middle age, old age, and death. We all go through each of these stages if we live long enough.

Do you remember being born, or earlier still being in your mother's womb, or earliest of all being conceived? Of course not, but the reality is that you experienced these things in your physical life.

You began when your mother and father had the sexual intercourse that resulted in your conception (yes, they did do that). Your father's sperm were ejaculated into the vagina of your mother and traveled up her vagina through the cervix and uterus and into the fallopian tube, where one of the sperm made a successful fusion with your mother's egg. At that moment, you became a zygote with the combined genes of both your father and mother, and then a blastocyst implanted in the uterine wall. From that point on, your new body began to form and grow. You developed in a cocoon of fluid and were nourished through your mother's umbilical cord. You were safe and warm inside her belly for nine months.

Then the trauma of birth began. Suddenly, the fluid surrounding you was gone and pressures were building. You found yourself slowly moving headfirst in a downward direction; you were being forcibly pushed out of your mother's body. As your head neared the exit, you began to experience your first exposure to light. And then you finally exited crying, or if not crying you were beaten until you did. You were wet and cold. Such was your welcoming into the harsh reality of the physical world.

You became a newborn, an infant, a rug rat, a toddler, and a terrible two-er, in that order. But you remember nothing of these early times (unlike your parents who would undoubtedly rather forget). You don't remember that you were constantly fed, clothed, bathed, and otherwise treated like royalty. Even your excretions were looked after (the most disgusting part for your parents).

Gradually you began to notice and interact with your physical environment. First there were bright colored and mobile toys that were placed above or in the crib where you were confined. You said your first word, you took your first step. And then you were off and running, constantly exploring the world around you while your parents went nearly out of their minds trying to keep you safe and out of trouble. They only bought you the safest of toys. Even the kitchen and other cabinet doors were secured so that you could not get your hands on some nasty chemical. Gates were placed to keep you out of certain areas or make sure that you did not fall down the stairs.

Then one day you had your first conscious thought. What a momentous event! Most of us will at least vaguely recall the occasion of our first awareness of self. One has to wonder why it takes so long for a human child to become self-aware. Perhaps we need the time to forget where we came from.

Now memories begin to collect, one after the other in an increasing flood. You may remember your first Christmas and the first time you went to kindergarten and then first grade. You recall the children you played with and the games you enjoyed with them. Early childhood is a happy time of life; some people say it was their happiest. Life is all play and discovery with no worries about the consequences or the future. Your parents take care of you, provide for you, and love you (although this is sadly not true for all children). The only "work" that you have is your school work and this is certainly not taxing in any great way at the early grade school level. And even this work disappears in the summers when school is out and life becomes all play again. On the other hand, your parents look forward to the Fall with bated breath.

Most people remember vignettes from their childhood. I know I do. It may be the first television program that you remember, or your first childhood friend, or the inside and backyard of your first home. I'll bet that many of you can remember the physical layout of that home, what the kitchen and living room and bedrooms and playroom and bathrooms were like and where they were in relation to each other. You may remember your backyard as well. The swing set, the grass, the trees, the neighbors houses. And of course you recall the interactions with your parents and relatives. They were all so large and impressive and commanding in your child's eyes.

At some point though, you began to feel your independence. This may have happened when you were given your first two-wheeled bike. Prior to that event, you were constrained to the locations in your neighborhood that were within walking or tricycle distance; that was your world. Your freedom was constrained to just a few blocks in all directions. But then one marvelous day the two-wheeler arrived, complete with its training wheels. After a number of runs around the block with the training wheels, guided and encouraged by one of your parents, you finally achieved the necessary balance to do without them. And when this happened, there was a rush of exhilaration! You now had the power to go much further afield on your own. You felt liberated, even though in actual fact your world was still constrained to only some of the streets in the immediate neighborhood. But it felt so good to be on that bike, to roam free to any place of your choosing that you were able to reach on your marvelous two-wheeled vehicle.

Yes, as one grows to be an older child, the world expands considerably. You start joining groups, things like little leagues and boy (or girl) scouts, and, as you progress in grade school, you participate in more and more school-sponsored events. There are field trips where you can see and do many new and exciting things. You roam further and further away from the safety of the neighborhood environs. You may travel on trains and boats and planes with family on vacations to distant places. And you start to interact more and more with people who are not your immediate family or relatives, and begin to notice that your childhood friends are not quite the same as you but different in many ways.

In middle school, unsettling changes take place that begin to generate an internal feeling of uneasiness. The subjects in school are starting to take on a higher level of depth and intensity and your parents encourage you to do well in them for the good of your future. Interestingly, and somewhat frighteningly, you also notice changes beginning in yourself. If you are a boy, you may start to feel strange stirrings at a location between your lower extremities. If you are a girl, you may notice that your chest is expanding significantly. Both boys and girls begin to have a strange attraction to each other. It's the end of the age of innocence.

By the time you get to high school, the hormones are raging. Girls do their best to attract boys and vice versa. Both genders want to explore their sexuality and there are sometimes unexpected and unfortunate ramifications, but this drive is so strong that caution is often thrown to the wind. This milieu may lead to self esteem difficulties, particularly for girls but also for boys. Peer pressure is intense.

The other thing that happens in high school is that greater pressures build to do well in academics. Parents begin telling their teenagers that they have to score good grades or they may not be able to get into college, and if they don't then their life will be significantly less than it could be. Teenagers tend to rebel against such pressures, naively believing that they know a great deal more than their overly concerned parents. They also think they are indestructible, which they are most assuredly not. Such are the difficult trials of the teenage years.

Once you survive the teenage nightmares, then you pass into young adulthood. There is an important choice to be made here, namely whether or not to attend college. If you do attend, you remain a student for a few more years dependent upon your parents at least for financial support if not for physical closeness. If you don't, then you must go out and seek employment in the cruel world, unfortunately with only a high school skill set. You have to start living in the real world. Those who do not go to college have to grow up much faster than those who do.

But if you attend college, you can postpone adulthood for at least a few more years. You might say that college represents the transition from teenager to young adult. You have more freedom and less dependence upon your parents who you likely no longer interact with on a daily basis. College is an opportunity to learn important job skills, but also an opportunity to learn important social skills. The environment is artificial, yet generally friendly and supportive. It is not the cruel world. Some college students spend most of their time partying and some focus almost all of their time on studying. However, the majority of students usually choose a suitable balance between the two.

After the typical four years of college, you are then faced with another important choice, whether to continue your higher education in graduate school or to go out and secure a job. Graduate school means that you can further postpone facing the real world for a little longer while you pursue your advanced degree. Getting a job means that you must make your real world entrance now, for better or worse.

For most people, maturity only really begins to develop near the end of the young adult years. What is maturity? Maturity is caring for others in addition to just yourself. Maturity is planning for the future rather than simply living for today. Getting your first job is a step towards maturity, but it doesn't mean you have become fully mature. Most young adults in their twenties are not very mature. They are driven to seek out adventure and new relationships. They want to explore the world and try as many new things as possible. Many young adults will get married sometime during their twenties. And then the two will go on exploring and discovering together, at least for a little while.

The game changer really happens when two people have their first child. Maturity and reality occur at a rapid pace then. It begins with the woman reporting to the man that she thinks she may be pregnant; this is followed by a visit to the doctor's office which confirms the fact. Then the baby planning phase starts, which is typically driven by the woman. It usually begins with the planning for the baby's room. We need this and we need that, so the couple goes out shopping for this-and-that. They buy the crib and the other accoutrements. They buy baby clothes, toys, and feeding implements. They spend endless hours rooting through the baby sections at the stores in the mall. The husband is typically bored silly, while the wife is filled with elation.

The baby grows within the mother. Soon all sex between husband and wife terminates for her fear of harming the fetus. She buys maternity clothes and starts to show more and more. Her body is changing in preparation for the birth; she suffers now and then from strange food cravings and the ills of morning sickness. The couple begins attending birthing classes with other couples who are in the same situation; learning how to breathe properly becomes a major focus. The woman's hormones change and she becomes more mellow. She makes frequent trips to the obstetrician.

Then after nine months, the big day finally arrives. Not always, but often, things start to happen either late at night or in the very early morning. The woman's water breaks and it is time for her husband, somewhat panic stricken but trying his best to control his anxiety, to rush her to the hospital for the birth. They get there and the woman begins her labor, with her husband at her side supporting her efforts. Nurses flurry in and out with supportive comments and much talk of dilating cervixes and the baby's vital signs. If all goes well, the baby arrives naturally in a few hours. If not, a caesarean section is often called for. In most instances, baby and mother come through this ordeal quite fine.

After a day or two, mother and baby come home. The husband and wife have now become a family. The husband will begin noticing that the wife's attention has shifted away from him and towards the baby. The newest member, boy or girl, requires constant attention both day and night. Nights are the worst, and the husband and wife share the night duties so that neither of them becomes too fatigued. There are a whole host of new chores and activities that descend upon husband and wife. Reality is really starting to bite.

You now have a major new set of responsibilities. Soon your family will outgrow your living accommodations and you will need to have a bigger living space, ideally a home with a backyard where the child (perhaps children by now) can play. You also need to focus on your career, so that you have a stable income to pay for your various home and family expenses. You must additionally start saving for the children's college education and, longer term, for your own eventual retirement.

Things revolve around family and home. You are involved with your childrens' education from grade school to middle school to high school and then to college. Your house needs constant upkeep and your career also makes demands on you. You need to devote adequate time to work activities to keep the money flowing in. The fun and games that you experienced as a childless couple are things of the distant past. Vacations, when they are possible, are cherished and savored. Life often seems to be an endless repetition of daily routines. This is not to say that your life is totally boring, there are certainly events that happen which make you happy and which you keep fondly stored in your long-term memory.

The next major change is when the children begin to leave the nest. The trigger for this is when they begin attending college and leave home to live in some college dorm usually far away. After college, they get jobs and apartments, and eventually may get married and start their own family lives. Once they all leave, it is just you and your spouse again. By this time you are middle-aged and thinking more and more about your retirement. Eventually, you do retire and then you may change your location, moving into a smaller place perhaps in a location where the weather is warm and pleasant most of the year.

How do you spend your time now? Some of it is spent communicating and worrying about your kids and their kids. How are they doing, what are they doing, are they happy and safe? Another part of your time may be spent trying to keep yourself physically active and healthy. So maybe you begin exercising on a more regular basis than you once did, and try eating healthier foods. You may also spend your time giving much more attention to interests and hobbies that you had little time for in your adult, family-raising years.

You hope you can maintain a good quality of life for as long as you can. For some people, this can be accomplished well into their 70's. But once you get to your 80's, you have definitely reached old age. Your body begins to break down more and more. You develop physical problems and illnesses that start to limit your activities and mobility. In addition, your mind begins to run slower and your thinking becomes less and less acute. Perhaps you find very old memories of long ago flashing into your mind, things you have not thought about for decades. Yet there they are, fresh and compelling because they take you back to the experiences of your youth.

And one day you die. If you have been able to live this long and not succumb to any earlier accident or illness, you will likely die in a hospital or a hospice. Relatives may or may not be present at the time of your death. But your body dies and your physical existence departs the world of matter. The key question though is—what happens to your consciousness?

Conscious Reality

When we are awake, we are all quite certain that we are conscious and living in the world of physical reality. In our dreams, we seem to go to distant places and have bizarre adventures, but upon awakening we always return to the same physical environment. However, it is important to realize that we only interact with the people and things around us through our senses and the sensory inputs supplied to the interpretive areas of our brain. Let's take a look at this in a little more detail.

We have five primary senses: sight, hearing, taste, smell, and touch. These senses provide the inputs to our brain that represent the physical environment around us.

How does sight work? We see with our eyes. The lens of the eye focuses the incoming light onto the retina at the back of the eye. The retina is covered with light-sensitive cells that are of two basic types, rods and cones. The cone cells are sensitive to color, while the rod cells are not. However, the rod cells have a higher sensitivity to light intensity than do the cone cells. These cells send electrical signals to the brain via the optic nerve at the back of the eye, and the brain then combines the signals from our two eyes into a single three-dimensional image. One may note that although the image on the retina is upside down because of the focusing action of the eye lens, the brain compensates and converts this image into a right-side-up image. The eye is only sensitive to a limited range of the electromagnetic spectrum; we can only see the color range from red to violet. This means that we only detect a limited range of the light energy that actually enters our eyes from the external environment.

Our ears provide the sense of hearing. The shape of the outer ear helps to focus sound wave signals from the environment into our inner ear. These signals hit the eardrum and it vibrates, transmitting acoustic signals to the inner ear components; these components are small bones which are relatively complex in shape. The small ear bones transfer the signals to the inner ear, which is a spiral-shaped chamber covered internally by nerve fibers that react to the vibrations and then send electrical impulses to the brain through the auditory nerve. The brain combines the inputs of our two ears to establish the direction and estimate the distance of the incoming sounds. We can hear sounds that are in the frequency range of approximately 16 to 28,000 cycles per second. As with sight, outside of this range we are not aware of the environmental sounds that may be occurring.

We experience the sense of taste with our taste buds, which are located on the tongue and the roof of our mouth. The basic tastes that we can detect are "sweet", "salty", "bitter", and "sour". The taste buds sensitive to "sweet" are located close to the tip of the tongue. The "bitter" buds are at the back of the tongue. The "salty" and "sour" taste buds are on the top and the side of the tongue. At the base of each taste bud is a nerve that sends the sensation of taste to the brain. It is somewhat difficult to quantify the range of tastes that can be detected, but this range clearly varies greatly with the individual. Some people have much more sensitive taste senses than do others, and such people often serve as "taste" testers for a wide range of foods and drinks.

Our nose serves as the body organ for the sense of smell. The nasal cavity is lined with mucous membranes that have smell receptor cells which are connected to the olfactory nerve. Basically, smells are generated by the vapors of various substances. Smell receptors can detect seven basic types of smells: camphor, musk, flower, mint, ether, acrid, and putrid. The smell receptor cells interact with the vapor molecules of the substance smelled, and then transmit electrical signals to the brain via the olfactory nerve. As with taste, different individuals have different sensitivities to smell. And dogs can sense odors at concentrations nearly 100 million times lower than humans can.

The sense of touch is communicated primarily through the skin. There are four touch sensations: cold, hot, contact, and pain. Nerves in the skin send these sensations to the brain; hairs on the skin can magnify the sensitivity. The concentration of touch nerves varies throughout the skin of the body. Fingertips and sexual organs have the highest concentrations of these nerve endings. The lightest touch that a person can feel is a pressure of about one-tenth of a pound per square inch.

One should note that we also possess secondary senses of balance and motion. These result from components located in the inner ear. There are three semi-circular canals there that are at approximately right angles to each other. These chambers are filled with a fluid that contains small particles, and the motion of these particles over small hair cells in the inner ear sends signals to the brain that the brain interprets as motion and acceleration.

Ultimately all of our sense organs send their electrical signal inputs to the brain for processing and interpretation. It is our brain that actually forms the reality we experience in physical life. The primary vision centers are located in the occipital lobe which is at the back of the brain and thus relatively far from the eyes themselves. It is at this location in the brain where we actually "see". The hearing centers are located in the temporal lobe. The temporal lobe is on the side of the head next to the location of the ears. Thus, the hearing centers are located relatively close to the auditory organs. The senses of taste and touch are formulated in the parietal lobe of the brain which is in the vicinity of the top of the head. Finally, our sense of smell appears to be formulated in the temporal lobe.

So everything we see, hear, smell, taste, and touch in the physical world is really a formulation that takes place inside our brain. It's important to recognize that what this means is that we cannot actually know in a completely objective way what the physical world is really like. The famous German philosopher Immanuel Kant was the first to realize this aspect of our physical reality.

Our brain is the formative organ of our conscious reality. Given that the brain is the formulator of what we can know about our physical reality, it is important to identify as much information as possible concerning how this formulation takes place.

One of the first people to probe the brain in a very direct way was Dr. Wilder Penfield, a Canadian neurosurgeon. His motivation was to use brain surgery to cure people of epilepsy and his approach was quite radical. He would open a patient's skull to expose the brain while the person was conscious and under only a local anesthetic. He would then touch an electrical probe to various locations on the surface of the brain and have the patient immediately verbally report what they felt. The purpose in doing this was to try and isolate the brain region associated with the epilepsy, so that he could then surgically remove that portion of the brain. Using these techniques, not only did Penfield help to treat epilepsy but he was also able to chart out many of the sensory locations in the brain. His charts are still used today for the study of brain function.

Penfield was also intensely interested in investigating the relationship of brain to consciousness and mind. He summarized much of this work in his book "The Mystery of the Mind", which was published a year before his death. In the book he reported that electrical stimulations of the brain could cause vivid memories to come to mind in the consciousness of his patients (1):

> It was evident at once that these were not dreams. They were electrical activations of the

sequential record of consciousness, a record that had been laid down during the patient's earlier experience. The patient "re-lived" all that he had been aware of in that earlier period of time as in a moving-picture "flashback".

On the first occasion, when one of these "flashbacks" was reported to me by a conscious patient (1933), I was incredulous. On each subsequent occasion, I marveled. For example, when a mother told me she was suddenly aware, as my electrode touched the cortex, of being in her kitchen listening to the voice of her little boy who was playing outside in the yard. She was aware of the neighborhood noises, such as passing motor cars, that might mean danger to him.

A young man stated he was sitting at a baseball game in a small town and watching a little boy crawl under the fence to join the audience. Another was in a concert hall listening to music. "An orchestration", he explained. He could hear the different instruments. All these were unimportant events, but recalled with complete detail.

D.F. could hear instruments playing a melody. I re-stimulated the same point thirty times trying to mislead her, and dictated each response to a stenographer. Each time I re-stimulated, she heard the melody again. It began at the same place and went on from chorus to verse. When she hummed an accompaniment to the music, the tempo was what would have been expected.

In his many years of brain neurosurgery, Wilder Penfield made the general observation that large amounts of the cerebral cortex could be removed without eliminating a person's consciousness. The fact is that a person can lead a relatively normal life even if they have only one-half of their brain. The brain is composed of two separate hemispheres which are joined together by a group of fibers called the corpus callosum. The left hemisphere controls the right side of your body. If you are a right-handed person, then your left hemisphere is considered to be the dominant one for you. Similarly, if you are left-handed, your right hemisphere is considered dominant. The left hemisphere is the location of logic and speech functions, while the right hemisphere is thought to be the primary area for creativity and emotions.

However, people can function reasonably well using only one hemisphere. This has been demonstrated quite conclusively by patients who have undergone the radical brain surgery called hemispherectomy. Hemispherectomy is the literal removal of one entire hemisphere of the brain, either the right hemisphere or the left hemisphere. Such radical surgery is only performed when there is no other recourse, such as cases of severe epilepsy or cancer on one side of the brain. Almost unbelievably, people who have this operation can function with near full normality even though they are walking around with one-half of their head literally empty! They are conscious, they can think, they can speak, they have all their senses (albeit there may be impairment in some of them). They also have motor functions on both sides of their body, again with some impairment but not major disability.

There is the case of the little girl who began having violent seizures at age three. The doctors diagnosed her with Rasmussen's syndrome which is a destruction of one side of her brain, in this case the right side. At age six, there was no alternative but to have a hemispherectomy, and her parents agreed. Surgeons spent seven hours carefully removing the right side of her brain. After the surgery, the left side of her body was paralyzed because her right brain was now gone. However, remarkably, after four weeks of intense physical therapy, she was able to walk out of the hospital. She returned to school and was a good student. The only lingering effects of the radical surgery were that she had to wear a brace on her left leg, and that she lost some peripheral vision. Other than that, she was a normal little girl again, albeit with a large cavity in the right side of her skull now filled with cerebrospinal fluid. Children are known to be medically quite elastic, and apparently her remaining left brain was quite able to assume almost all of the normal full-brain functions.

There is also the case of the middle-aged man who had to have his cancerous left hemisphere removed. The left hemisphere contains the centers for speech, as well as reading and writing. Yet in this case, after eight months of recovery, he was able to speak intelligibly in short phrases and walk with the assistance of a cane. Although he was previously a right-handed person, he learned to become left-handed, and his right brain was able to accommodate his speech functions to a significant extent.

These hemispherectomy cases are totally remarkable and clearly beg the question: Does each of us really have two brains inside our heads? Why do we have two brain hemispheres that, if needed, can be reduced to only one? Having two hemispheres is not a necessary condition for our consciousness and functioning.

The cases of people who have had their corpus callosum deliberately severed for medical reasons in the treatment of severe epilepsy are most interesting. This dramatic medical procedure basically isolates the right hemisphere from the left hemisphere. When this is done, visual information no longer moves between the two sides of the brain. If an image is presented to the right visual field (that is, to the left hemisphere which is where information from the right field is processed) patients can describe what they saw. But when the same image is displayed to the left visual field, patients say that they do not see anything. However, if they are asked to point to an object similar to the one being projected, they are able to do so with ease. Their right brain sees the image and can mobilize a nonverbal response but it cannot talk about what it saw. The same kind of finding proves true for the senses of touch, smell and sound. With regard to motor control, each half of the brain can control the upper muscles of both arms, but the muscles manipulating hand and finger movement can only be controlled by one hemisphere; the right hemisphere controls only the left hand and the left hemisphere only the right hand. It has been observed that the two hemispheres direct significantly different aspects of thought and action. Each half has its own specialization and its own limitations and advantages. The left brain is dominant for language and speech while the right brain is best at visual-motor tasks. This has caused people to generalize that writers are left-brained and visual artists are right-brained.

In one corpus callosum severance patient, his right hemisphere was more developed in language ability before the operation. This allowed researchers to interview both sides of his split brain. When the researchers asked the right side what he wanted to be, he answered an automobile racer while his left side stated he wanted to be a draftsman. Another patient also exhibited strange behaviors with his right and left hands. His right hand was trying to pull up his pants while the left hand was trying to pull then down. A similar incident occurred when a split-brain patient was having an argument with his wife. The patient was attacking his wife with his left hand while his right hand was defending her. It almost seems as though there were two conscious entities existing in the one body of such patients.

Then there is the strange case of Clive Wearing, the man who lives in the Now. Wearing was born in 1938 and is an accomplished musician. On March 29, 1985, he contracted herpes encephalitis, and the virus attacked his brain, damaged the hippocampus, which plays a major role in the handling of long term memory formation.

Because of this, Wearing developed a profound case of total amnesia as a result of his illness. Since the part of the brain required to transfer memories from the 'working' to the 'long term' area was damaged, he is completely unable to encode new memories. He spends every day "waking up" every few minutes and "restarting" his consciousness once the time span of his short term memory elapses. He remembers very little of his life before 1985, but his love for his second wife Deborah, whom he married the year prior to his illness, is undiminished. In fact, he greets her joyously each time they meet, thinking that he has not seen her in years, although she may have just left the room to bring him a glass of water. Despite having major retrograde as well as anterograde amnesia, and thus only a moment-to-moment consciousness, Wearing still remembers how to play the piano and conduct a choir, despite having no recollection of having received a musical education.

In a daily diary which he keeps, each page is filled with entries similar to the following:

> *8:31 AM: Now I am really, completely awake.*
> *9:06 AM: Now I am perfectly, overwhelmingly awake.*
> *9:34 AM: Now I am superlatively, actually awake.*

When asked if he ever has any dreams when he is sleeping, Wearing stated that he never dreams. Clearly, this man is someone who is quite literally living in, or better said, trapped in the Now.

What happens to the brain and consciousness when a person has a stroke? A first hand account of this situation is given by neuroanatomist Jill Taylor in her book "My Stroke of Insight" (2). On the morning of December 10, 1996 Jill Taylor suffered a stroke at her home while preparing to go to work. It began with a sharp pain behind her left eye and was followed by weakness and disorientation. She knew something was wrong, but she didn't immediately know what, so she showered and dressed. But when her right arm became paralyzed she realized that she was having a stroke. She had the following thought at this time (2):

> *Wow, how many scientists have the opportunity to study their own brain function and mental deterioration from the inside out?*

Yes, that was indeed the position she was in. A blood vessel had burst in the left hemisphere of her brain which affected a number of brain functions in her motor cortex, sensory cortex, orientation association cortex, and speech cortex. She was losing her ability to move, sense the world, relate to time and space, and create as well as understand speech. She needed help, and fast.

But Jill was finding it more and more difficult to think logically and to plan how to go about getting help. After much intense mental effort, she decided to try and call a colleague at her place of work. But the problem was she couldn't remember the telephone number. However, blessedly the phone number eventually entered her consciousness. The brain hemorrhage was affecting her mathematical abilities, so when she wrote down the individual numbers that appeared in her mind, they just looked like "squiggles" on the sheet of paper. Fortunately, she was able to match these "squiggles" with the same "squiggles" that appeared on the phone keypad, and she succeeded in making the call.

Then she faced another significant challenge. When the phone was answered on the other end, her mind tried to say *"This is Jill, I need help"*. But the speech that she heard come out of her mouth was unintelligible, and so were the words that the person on the other end of the phone said in response. Very fortunately, her colleague recognized her phone number on his end and realized that the gibberish he was hearing from her voice meant she was in trouble and needed help. So he came over to her apartment and from that point on she got the medical help that she needed so desperately.

Jill was indeed presented a unique opportunity. To directly observe the functioning of her mind when the left hemisphere of her brain was almost totally incapacitated and disfunctional. What she discovered was that her ego, the material-centered neuroanatomist Dr. Jill Taylor and all the baggage that went with it, was now gone. It was replaced by something else and that something else was associated with her right hemisphere which was undamaged and completely functional. Here is how she described it (2):

> *My entire self-concept shifted as I no longer perceived myself as a single, a solid, an entity with boundaries that separated me from the entities around me. I understood that at the most elementary level, I am a fluid. Of course I am a fluid! Everything around us, about us, among us, within us, and between us is made up of atoms and molecules vibrating in space. Although the ego center of our language center prefers defining our self as individual and solid, most of us are aware that we are made up of trillions of cells, gallons of water, and ultimately everything about us exists in a constant and dynamic state of activity. My left hemisphere*

> *had been trained to perceive myself as a solid,*
> *separate from others. Now, released from*
> *that restrictive circuitry, my right hemisphere*
> *relished in its attachment to the eternal flow. I*
> *was no longer isolated and alone. My soul was*
> *as big as the universe and frolicked with glee in*
> *a boundless sea.*

Three days after her stroke, Jill's mother arrived at her hospital room in Boston. When she was told that her mother would be arriving, Jill had to spend mental energy just trying to understand what the concept of "mother" meant. But it did come back to her. Her mother quickly became Jill's primary nurse and caregiver, and was of immense help in her recovery.

The medical diagnosis was that Jill's brain hemorrhage was the result of an arteriovenous malformation (AVM) in her left hemisphere. It was recommended that she have craniotomy surgery to remove the remnants of the AVM as well as a remnant clot the size of a golf ball in her brain. If this were not done, there was a good chance that she would have another brain hemorrhage which might be fatal the next time.

Five days after the stroke, Jill went home to her apartment with her mother as her caregiver. Jill's mother basically had to teach her how to think again with her left hemisphere. She taught Jill about the concept of color with jigsaw puzzles and she began teaching her to read again with little children's books. She also nursed Jill to be strong enough to endure her brain surgery operation.

The operation took place on December 27, 1996 at Massachusetts General Hospital in Boston. When Jill woke up from the operation, she said that she felt like "me" again. She also had a nine inch "U" shaped stitched-up scar on the left side of her head where the surgeon had gone in for the operation. Five days after the operation, she was discharged from the hospital.

Several months prior to her stroke, Jill had agreed to give a technical presentation on neuroanatomy at Fitchburg State College. She made it her goal to give this 20 minute presentation in such a manner that the audience would not realize that she was actually recovering from a major stroke. However, because of the stroke damage to her left hemisphere, the reality was that she was no longer an expert in neuroanatomy since she had lost much of her technical knowledge. So her course of action was to draw enough information from her previous talks to be able to give this presentation. She practiced the 20 minute talk over and over for a month until she was proficient at presenting it, albeit somewhat robotically. And she pulled it off successfully; her Fitchburg talk went fine. This must be considered an astounding accomplishment for her, taking place as it did so soon after a major stroke.

However Jill's complete recover was a long one, taking eight years in total. She was not able to function in her old job, so she moved to Indiana to be closer to her parents. Two years after her stroke, her brain again became capable of retaining large amounts of information and she began teaching courses in Anatomy/Physiology and Neuroscience at the Rose Hulman Institute of

Technology in Terre Haute, Indiana. It took four years of physical training for her to be able to walk with a smooth rhythm. At the fourth year, her mind again became able to multitask; prior to that she was only able to perform one task at a time. Jill's mathematical skills had been severely impaired by the stroke. It wasn't until year five that she was able to do long division again. During her eighth year of recovery, Jill's perception of herself finally changed from that of being a fluid back to that of being a solid. At the present time, Jill teaches Neuroanatomy and Gross Anatomy to medical students at the Indiana University School of Medicine and also travels for the Harvard Brain Bank as the "Singin' Scientist". She had made a truly astounding recovery.

Yes, Jill's experience is remarkable. She has been able to obtain insights about her brain from the inside-out. Here is how she summarized her "stroke of insight" (2):

> *My stroke of insight is that at the core of my right hemisphere consciousness is a character that is directly connected to my feeling of deep inner peace. It is completely committed to the expression of peace, love, joy, and compassion in the world.*

Based on what she has written in her book, Jill was not the same person after her stroke. She indicated that *"the portion of my character that was stubborn, arrogant, sarcastic, and/or jealous resided within the ego center of that wounded left brain"*. Upon her recovery, she was able to eliminate many of these negative aspects from her left hemisphere thinking. She became more right-brained and realized that her true self was part of a larger, eternal cosmic flow. She quite literally had a stroke of sublime insight.

How does the brain experience the reality of the sensory inputs it receives? It seems to our experience that our sensory vision of the external world is immediate in nature. When something happens to us, we see it or feel it in real time. But is this actually true?

This question has been explored in considerable detail by the seminal work of Benjamin Libet. Libet was a neurophysiologist at the University of California School of Medicine in San Francisco. In the late 1950's, he began collaborations with a brain surgeon who had developed a surgical technique to control the tremors, tics and spasms caused by Parkinson's disease. This technique involved the implantation of electrodes directly into the brain to stop the tremors at their source. Since the brain feels no pain, the surgery was done under local anesthetic and the patients were fully conscious during the surgery. A coin-sized hole was drilled through the skull to expose the motor centers of the brain that control the sense of touch. With the consent of the patients, Libet inserted an extra electrode through which he could introduce a small amount of electrical current and then have the patients describe what sort of stimulus they felt.

What Libet found was that he could only generate a sensory reaction from the fully awake patients if he induced a pulsed current (3). The frequency of these electrical pulses or their polarity had little influence. With gentle pulsing current, the patients reported relatively specific feelings, such as a drop of water trickling down the back of their hand. However, if the magnitude of the current was increased, these specific feelings turned into just a tingling sensation. Libet observed that the length of time of the electrical pulse train was important to the patient being able to report any sensation at all. If the pulse train were less than approximately 500 milliseconds (one-half a second), the patient would report no induced feeling, but if it were greater than 500 milliseconds, then the patient would "feel" it.

This was a very intriguing result because it seems to indicate that we experience real-world events in our consciousness about one-half a second after they actually occur in real time. Such a result is counter intuitive to our common sense experience of things. When we touch something with our finger, it does not seem to us that there is a half-second delay in our awareness of the touch. Rather, it seems that our awareness is almost simultaneous with the actual touch.

Libet realized that he needed to reference his time results to a base time and for this he chose the technique of "evoked response potentials" (ERPs). The evoked response potential is essentially an elecroencephalographic (EEG) methodology that isolates individual sensory brain wave signals. Normally, evoked response potentials are recorded by placing electrodes on the surface of the scalp, but since he had access to the brain, Libet placed his ERP electrodes directly on the surface of the brain, where these signals are exceptionally sharp and well-defined.

For an ERP stimulus, Libet employed a brief electrical shock induced on the back of the patient's hand. In the ERP, he noted an initial large spike at approximately 80 milliseconds which was the result of the nerve signal from the hand traveling to the brain location being monitored for the ERP. However, after this spike the ERP signal did not drop to zero but instead continued at a lower level for approximately 500 milliseconds. Libet interpreted this extended ERP signal as the brain processing required to produce a conscious sensation of the stimulus. What was quite remarkable, however, was that the awake patients actually reported feeling the stimulus after only an 80 millisecond period, rather than after a 500 millisecond period. In other words, the patients said that they felt the stimulus almost simultaneously, while the ERP results indicated that the stimulus really came into their consciousness only after a much longer 500 millisecond time period.

How could this be resolved? Libet's interpretation was that the brain was artificially antedating the conscious recall of the event time from the actual 500 millisecond delay time to the 80 millisecond delay time, and he conducted a series of experiments that seem to confirm this explanation. However, he offered no mechanism by which the brain could produce such an unusual effect.

So does reality actually take place one-half of a second before we are consciously aware of it? Libet's data are compelling, but a number of other researchers have questioned his interpretation of the raw data. Until a mechanism is clearly identified to show how the brain could antedate these time events, the jury is still out on this important reality question.

Another series of experiments that Libet conducted had to do with the subject of free will. Now, free will is a very interesting subject indeed for experimental brain studies. These studies did not involve the implanting of electrodes into the brain as was the case with his previous experiments on consciousness, but rather the monitoring of ERP signals recorded on the scalps of the test subjects. The test subjects themselves were college students. These students were seated in front of a clock-type face that went through a full 360 degree revolution in the space of 2.56 seconds, rather than 60 seconds. They were then instructed to look at the clock face and remember the clock hand position when they first had a conscious thought to make a move of their wrist or finger. Using this experimental arrangement, Libet could measure both the time of the ERP signal on the scalp for the wrist or finger movement, and the time that the subjects felt that they made the conscious decision to move their wrist or finger.

What Libet observed was that the conscious decision to make the movement took place 200 milliseconds before the actual physical motion, but that the ERP signal on the scalp recording this motion in the brain took place 500 milliseconds before the actual motion (4). This result suggests that the brain activity to make the motion began much before the conscious free will decision to make the movement. Needless to say, this was a very profound experimental observation related to the reality (or the non-reality) of what we call free will.

Now, we all intuitively feel that we have free will in association with our conscious actions. We make the conscious decision to do something and then we do it. We are the ones in control of our conscious actions. But Libet's results suggest is that we are not really in control of even the simplest actions, such as moving a finger. However, Libet himself provided a way to still preserve free will given his experimental results. He said that within the 300 millisecond timeframe of the unconscious start of the action and the conscious realization of wanting to act, the person still had a free will capability to veto the action.

Libet's free will experiments have been much debated since he first performed them. A number of people take them to mean that our conscious awareness plays absolutely no role in our actions, that our actions are all dictated by processes that take place at the subconscious brain level. Obviously, this has major implications for the morality of our actions. If a person makes the decision to murder someone in cold blood, then they could say that he really had no conscious free will control of this decision, that it was made by his subconscious, and that his conscious will had no involvement at all. Think of the ramifications of this for society's criminal system. Essentially it would say that no one is really responsible for criminal actions, or any other actions for that matter.

Scientists continue to refine the research based on Libet's free will experiments. Recently, studies have been performed where electrodes were inserted into living human brains to record the activity of individual neurons (5). The primary reason for doing this was to pin down the brain neuronal location of debilitating epileptic seizures so that this bit of brain matter could then be surgically removed. However, between the times of these seizures, the patients volunteered for studies conducted to determine what the individual neurons were actually controlling. Twelve patients were employed and a total of 1019 neurons were recorded.

The patients were instructed to gaze at a Libet-type clock face and remember the clock position when they made the conscious decision to press a button. What was found was that about a quarter of the neurons being monitored in the supplementary motor area of the frontal lobe of the brain registered significant neuronic activity 700 milliseconds before the conscious decision. Thus it would seem that Libet's result has been verified down to the level of individual brain neurons.

Drugs are something that can affect the brain's perception of reality. Foremost in this regard is the drug LSD. The chemical name of LSD is lysergic acid diethylamide. It was first synthesized in 1938 by the Swiss chemist Albert Hofmann, and was produced and sold by Sandoz Laboratories in Switzerland starting in 1947. LSD is colorless and odorless, and is typically taken on blotter paper or in a sugar cube. The chemical is extremely potent, and the threshold dose for observable effects is only 20-30 micrograms, a very tiny amount. LSD produces an altered state of consciousness when ingested and was considered as a potential psychiatric drug in the 1950s and 1960s.

The effects of LSD were first noticed by its discoverer, Albert Hofmann, five years after its synthesis when he accidentally ingested a small amount of the powerful drug. Here is Hofmann's account of the accidental discovery (6):

> *In the final step of the synthesis, during the*
> *purification and crystallization of lysergic acid*

diethylamide in the form of a tartrate (tartaric acid salt), I was interrupted in my work by unusual sensations. The following description of this incident comes from the report that I sent at the time to Professor Stoll:

Last Friday, April 16, 1943, I was forced to interrupt my work in the laboratory in the middle of the afternoon and proceed home, being affected by a remarkable restlessness, combined with a slight dizziness. At home I lay down and sank into a not unpleasant intoxicated-like condition, characterized by an extremely stimulated imagination. In a dreamlike state, with eyes closed (I found the daylight to be unpleasantly glaring), I perceived an uninterrupted stream of fantastic pictures, extraordinary shapes with intense, kaleidoscopic play of colors. After some two hours this condition faded away.

Because of its effects, the CIA began experimenting with LSD in the 1950s to investigate its possible use in their clandestine operations. Most often, LSD was given to test subjects without their knowledge, so that its effects could be observed by CIA personnel. This was called Project MK-ULTRA. Rather interestingly, the records of MK-ULTRA were destroyed in 1973 at the direction of then CIA Director Richard Helms, making it difficult to know the entire scope of the project. There were a number of deaths associated with this CIA project. The best known is that of Frank Olson, a U.S. Army biochemist and biological researcher. In November 1953,

Olson was unknowingly given a dose of LSD. One week later he jumped out the window of a New York City hotel and fell thirteen stories to his death. His death, originally attributed as a suicide, was later indicated to be a result of negative effects of his LSD dose.

In the 1960s, then Harvard professor Timothy Leary began experiments with LSD that were initially targeted at its potential beneficial psychiatric effects. Rather unfortunately, these initial legitimate studies propagated in a major way into the hippie counterculture, with Leary as a guru advocating that young people "turn on, tune in, drop out". The "turn on" part involved drug usage, of which LSD played a major role. These negative aspects led to a 1968 decision by the U.S. government to make LSD an illegal drug. Because of this action, genuine research work on the effects of LSD on the brain came to an abrupt halt, and research is only now beginning to resume again under carefully controlled conditions.

So what are the effects of LSD that caused such a stir in the past? They are profound indeed. As was mentioned, only minute amounts of LSD can produce a major alteration in the conscious perception of the brain. Here is a clinical summary of LSD effects that was reported in a scientific publication in 1962 (7). The test subjects were given doses of 100-225 micrograms of LSD, and its effects began about one-half hour after ingestion and continued for eight hours thereafter.

> We may now summarize the outstanding
> effects of LSD-25 on the present sample. Our
> subjects experienced loss of control in a number

of areas and many were frightened or angry at themselves as a result of this loss. In respect to thinking, loss of voluntary control over attention and impaired functioning were prominent. Our subjects felt that their bodies were affected physically (primarily due to autonomic changes) and also reported disturbed motility and bodily transformations. They experienced loss of emotional control, in such varied forms as fear, anger or elation. Their feeling of contact with reality broke down, and in some subjects, perceptual distortions occurred.

This rather dry summary of LSD's effects does not really communicate its dramatic effects on an individual. A much more descriptive and visceral account of LSD's effects may be found in the online-published book "LSD-Revelation of the Mind" (8). Here is a more graphic summary of what people may experience under the influence of LSD:

The first effects of the LSD are likely to be physical changes in how your body feels and visual changes in what you see and how you see it.

Let's start with the physical changes involving how your body feels. People don't realize how physical the experience will be. It will likely start with a tingling feeling, maybe in your fingertips and other parts of your body, simultaneously. It will be a tingling, vibrating, throbbing kind of feeling and you will feel sensations throughout your body that you have never felt before.

You might feel like you're all charged up with energy. It might feel like delicate threads, electrical forces or powerful currents of energy radiating, rippling, flowing, pulsing, surging or streaming throughout the body.

It's even possible to feel the blood moving through the veins or become conscious of your cells as alive and active. Your body can feel so light that it's as if you're floating in the air or your body can feel like it weighs ten tons and that it would take tremendous effort just to stand up.

There are other changes that can be happening with your body. It's possible to feel as if your body is made of another substance. It can feel like your body is made of wood, glass, plastic, metal, marble, stone, clay, paper, leather or anything else.

You can actually become an inanimate object or even an imaginary object, a robot, a plant, an animal, pure energy, the earth, air, fire, water or anything. If you become a plant or an animal, you will be tuned into the consciousness of the plant or animal. This is even the case if you become an object, like a piece of wood.

Another aspect of the physical changes is the sense of touch. All of the senses are incredibly intensified and we'll get to that later. For now, just staying with the sense of touch, it becomes electric, erotic, sensual and full of pleasure.

The experience of not having a body is a little different. Be assured that you have your body the whole time no matter what seems to be happening, even if it seems like you and your body are dissolving and disappearing.

Another interpretation of having no body is to not feel the body. You know that your body is still there somehow, but it's like you're floating in a sensuous sea of joy, ecstasy and bliss.

You will see objects that are usually seen as still, now moving in some way. It's not that an object is moving to a different part of the room. It's much more likely that the object is in the same spot, but it's slowly vibrating or expanding and contracting or seems to be breathing in and out.

From the LSD perspective, when you see the object, you are not thinking about or keying on what its use or function is. If you are looking at a chair, you know that it's a chair but you are thinking about how beautiful, significant and meaningful in itself that the chair is.

It's like you can perceive the nature, significance or "meaning" of the object, beyond its usual function and realize that there is nothing inferior about a pencil being a pencil and not a person. The pencil has its own dignity in being a pencil.

You can tune in to what seems to be the consciousness of an object and how it thinks and feels. This may sound to you like it's too much or going too far if I'm saying that ordinary objects have deep significance, meaning and beauty, that they are alive with a consciousness that thinks and feels in its own way and that you can get tuned into all of this with LSD. Actually, it makes a lot of sense but it will take a lot of explaining.

An object is a part of the universe meaning a part of your full identity. You are different than the object but ultimately not separate from it the way arms and legs are different but not separate from the body. When you are tripping and the interfering ego is finally out of your way, then you can become aware of that connection between you and an object, that the object is a part of you and that you are a part of the object. A person and an object are a part of each other because they both have the same full identity, which is the entire universe. It's like the person is an arm, the object is a leg and the entire universe is the body.

The concept of time is interesting. Time is usually thought of in terms of seconds, minutes and hours or past, present and future. During an LSD experience, you are way beyond all of *that. You're no longer in clock time. You're in real time. You can look at a clock and it might as well be on another planet because whatever the clock says doesn't mean anything now. Any amount of clock time will seem like it's a much much longer amount of time.*

For example, John can go outside the door and come right back in. Bob, who is tripping, may ask John what took so long or why he was gone for such a long time, when it was really just for a moment. Another example would be someone smoking a cigarette and it seems to them as if they've been smoking if for hours and they haven't even needed to go to the ashtray yet.

What's happening is that time is getting extended to the point that it's irrelevant and doesn't exist anymore. You now have all the time in the world. You are in eternity. Sometimes people think of eternity as something that goes on millennium after millennium, forever and ever. Obviously, that can't happen because, unfortunately, you will eventually have to come down and the trip will be over. While you are tripping, though, it seems as if it will go on forever and that feeling of eternity is very real. Eternity means that you're not in clock time, but real time or eternal time or real, eternal time or eternal, real time or simply, eternity.

There is nothing but the present. When someone is tripping, it's clear that yesterday and tomorrow are meaningless and that here and now is everything.

With LSD, when time is extended and you are in eternity, the mental processes are speeded up. You are experiencing so much more in a minute of clock time than usual that it seems as if it could not possibly have been only 1 minute.

Along with the timeless, eternal flavor to everything, there is also a richness, radiance, magic and beauty to everything. Combining all of this with feeling physically greater than ever and it sounds a little more like heaven. The magnitude, quality and richness of LSD consciousness is genuinely magnificent far beyond compare, far beyond anything previously experienced and far beyond the wildest fantasies of anyone's imagination before they have had LSD. What happens during an LSD experience is more real than real. What we think of as real is just that tiny fraction of 1 percent of reality. Anything more than that, even if it's only a larger fraction of 1 percent, could be called more real than real. This "more real than real" concept is significant.

An important feature of the LSD experience is dramatically increased, expanded and widened perception and awareness, along with sharpened, heightened intensification of the senses. The senses will be operating differently than what you are used to. It will be like you are seeing for the first time or seeing clearly for the first time. It will also be like you are hearing, smelling, touching and tasting for the first time, indeed, living for the first time. That's how incredible it all is. It's the first time you are able to experience all of the senses simultaneously operating at full efficiency.

Consciousness itself becomes enlarged, widened, expanded and has a dreamlike, spacy character, but the mind is more clear and alert than ever.

Like with everything else, when you listen to music, it will be like you are hearing it for the first time. No matter how many times you have heard a certain song and how familiar you are with it, with LSD it will be like you have never heard it before or never heard it like this before.

A person might look at their fingers and instead of 10 fingers, they see hundreds of them. It's nothing to worry about. You know that it's just 10 fingers. The fingers or any part of the body can be seen as getting bigger or smaller, growing or shrinking. One finger might be getting bigger and another finger getting smaller. One hand may be a lot bigger than the other. An arm or a leg may become very, very long or get so small that it's hardly there. If you stick your arm way out and make a fist, it can look like the fist is a mile away or it can look as if your nose is a fraction of an inch away the fist.

One may perceive themselves as only 3 inches tall and try to hide behind a pack of cigarettes. If someone is experiencing being 3 inches tall, they might "worry" that someone will step on them and they will get crushed. Trying to cross the street can be too "dangerous" and the person will ask a companion to pick them up and hold them in their hand. If you see yourself as only 3 inches tall, then the room you're in and the other people will seem gigantic.

If it's the other way and the body seems to be getting bigger, the person may be "concerned" that their body will burst through the walls and crush everything, including the other people. It may be that you are the giant and everyone else is 3 inches tall.

The whole room itself can seem to be expanding or contracting or be breathing in and out, just like a single object can seem to be doing that. The objects and the entire room can be doing all of this according to how you think and feel. If your mood or thoughts change, the "action" in the room and of the room can change and if music comes on, then the objects may start singing and dancing, with the room vibrating or flowing to the music.

With LSD, your vision is very fine tuned. You can look at a painting and notice the thickness of the paint or look at some-thing written in ink and see the thickness of the ink. You may not be able to read, though, because the letters of the words might jump around, change shapes, merge into each other, etc. Even if the letters and words are not "behaving" so wildly, so that it's possible to read, you are way beyond all of this.

The inanimate objects are alive and if you hold something in your hand, you can feel the aliveness of the object. It can even be unclear where the skin of your hand ends and the object begins, as if they are merged with each other.

You can look at an object and see everything down to the finest details that you never noticed before, as if your eyes are almost microscopes. If you look at a piece of wood, you can see the texture and the grain patterns of the wood will wiggle wildly.

When you take LSD, it will be like seeing color for the first time, as if your entire life before was in black and white. In a similar way, with LSD, it's like you are alive for the first time, as if your entire life before was lived as a statue. People think that they are already living, alive and in color, but if we are aware of only a tiny fraction of one percent of the brain, it's fair to say that this is a society of statues disguised as people, sleepwalking in a black and white world.

You are seeing all these colors in movement, in harmony, all in the same flow, rhythm or pattern and you can feel the same flow, rhythm or pattern within you.

With LSD, color, like everything else, becomes tremendously intensified. You will see the brightest, most radiant, brilliant and beautiful colors by far that you have ever seen. The colors will shine, sparkle and glow like diamonds. The living, moving colors will be spectacular and electrifyingly exciting

Objects will seem as if they have their own light coming from inside. The object, its colors and the light are all alive, moving, dancing, wiggling, merging, changing, etc.

The lights and colors of the Las Vegas strip are like a power failure compared to what you can see with your eyes closed, while tripping.

There is no telling exactly what you will see once you get past the moving, changing, living clouds of color or the moving, changing, living geometric designs of color. You may see scenes or events from the historical past, both of your own personal past or the historical past of man or even the historical past of all life and all existence and believe it or not, all of that is stored in your brain!

When you see all of this with your eyes closed, you aren't just seeing it, but it's as if you are living it. The visions are so vividly clear, the details so intricate, the light so brilliant, the colors so radiantly dazzling, the people and places so real that you know that this is ultimately meaningful and significant. Everything here is on an ultimate level. If you see an ancient temple with glowing jewels and colors everywhere, you know that this is the home of the gods, that you are one of them, that you belong there and you do.

At some point, you realize that this is heaven and paradise. The way it may happen is that you will be getting visions and suddenly, there is just a bright light. All you see is this brilliant light. It might be white or yellow or all of the colors, like a rainbow is all the colors. It's not just a light and there is no further way to explain this with words, but you know that this is God, that this is where you came from and where you'll go later. This "light" may engulf you so that you are merged or united with God or ultimate reality. This is the religious experience of realizing that the ego really is, without any doubt, just that tiny fraction of one percent and that this, now, is your real, original, full, ultimate identity. You are in heaven and at home. Heaven is our original home.

This rather lengthy description of an LSD trip has been rendered to give the reader a more complete appreciation of what the "mind-blowing" effects of LSD actually are for the experiencer. But how is this type of vivid experience produced by the effects of LSD on the chemistry of the brain? The answer is no one really has a good idea at present. A major reason for this is the fact that genuine research on the effects of LSD on the brain have been so severely curtailed since it was declared an illegal drug.

What is known is that LSD seems to affect the serotonergic system in the brain. However, the actual mechanisms by which it acts on that system to modify behavior remain unclear. Serotonin is a neurotransmitter and although serotonin is only produced by a small number of neurons (1000's), each of those neurons innervates as many as 500,000 other neurons. The best current scientific explanation is that LSD may trigger a cascading release of serotonin and other neurotransmitters in the brain, resulting in heightened neural activity that the conscious mind then struggles to interpret sensibly, resulting in altered perceptions, effects, and hallucinations. Some researchers theorize that LSD blocks serotonin receptors, while others speculate that LSD intensifies them; the most widely accepted theory is that LSD does both, blocking certain receptors and stimulating others. But no one really knows for sure.

The effects of LSD appear to have elements in common with the symptoms of the mental disorders of psychosis and schizophrenia.

The word "psychosis" was first put forward in 1845 as an alternative description for behaviors previously described as "madness". Psychosis was thought to be associated with the mind, while neurosis was considered related to the nervous system. The major divisions of psychosis are bipolar disorder (manic depression) and dementia (schizophrenia). People who have psychosis often report hallucinations or delusional beliefs, and may exhibit personality changes and thought disorder, which can also be accompanied by unusual or bizarre behavior. Their thought processes seem not right. They may have unfounded fears that people are out to do them harm or that rather ordinary events are dangerous for them. They may hear voices or see things that are not there. A person in a psychotic episode may run down a long hallway at full speed with their eyes closed. It may sometimes seem that a psychotic person acts as though they "were possessed by the devil".

The major symptoms of schizophrenia are hallucinations, delusions, thought disorders, and movement disorders. Hallucinations are things a person sees, hears, smells, or feels that no one else can see, hear, smell, or feel. "Voices" are the most common type of hallucination in schizophrenia; many people with the disorder say they hear voices. The voices may talk to the person about his or her behavior, order the person to do certain things, or warn the person of danger. Sometimes the voices talk to each other. People with schizophrenia may hear voices for a long time before family and friends finally begin to notice the problem. Other types of hallucinations include seeing people or objects that are not there, smelling odors that no one else detects, and feeling things like invisible fingers touching their bodies when no one is near.

Delusions are false beliefs that a person holds to even after other people prove that these beliefs are not true or logical. People with schizophrenia can have delusions that seem bizarre, such as thinking that the neighbors can control the person's behavior with magnetic waves. They may also believe that people on television are directing special messages to them, or that radio stations are broadcasting their thoughts aloud to others. Sometimes they believe they are someone else, such as a famous historical figure. They may have paranoid delusions and believe that others are trying to harm them, such as by cheating, harassing, poisoning, spying on, or plotting against them or the people they care about. These beliefs are called delusions of persecution. For example, there was the case of a delusional woman who believed that her husband of thirty years had somehow changed into a complete stranger and was now a threat to her.

Thought disorders are unusual or dysfunctional ways of thinking. One form of thought disorder is called disorganized thinking. This is when a person has trouble organizing his or her thoughts or connecting them logically. They may talk in a garbled way that is hard to understand. Another form is called thought blocking. In this case a person stops speaking abruptly in the middle of a thought. When asked why he or she stopped talking, the person may say that it felt as if the thought had been taken out of his or her head. Finally, a person with a thought disorder might make up meaningless words, or neologisms.

Movement disorders often appear as agitated body movements. A person with a movement disorder may repeat certain motions over and over. At the other extreme, a person may become catatonic. Catatonia is a state in which a person does not move or respond to others.

Perhaps the most well-known case of schizophrenia is that of the 1994 Nobel Prize-winning mathematician John

Nash. The case of John Nash was the subject of the popular movie "A Beautiful Mind". Here is how Nash described his schizophrenia in his Nobel Prize autobiography (9):

> Now I must arrive at the time of my change from scientific rationality of thinking into the delusional thinking characteristic of persons who are psychiatrically diagnosed as "schizophrenic" or "paranoid schizophrenic". But I will not really attempt to describe this long period of time but rather avoid embarrassment by simply omitting to give the details of truly personal type.

> While I was on the academic sabbatical of 1956-1957 I also entered into marriage. Alicia had graduated as a physics major from M.I.T. where we had met and she had a job in the New York City area in 1956-1957. She had been born in El Salvador but came at an early age to the U.S. and she and her parents had long been U.S. citizens, her father being an M. D. and ultimately employed at a hospital operated by the federal government in Maryland.

> The mental disturbances originated in the early months of 1959 at a time when Alicia happened to be pregnant. And as a consequence I resigned my position as a faculty member at M.I.T. and, ultimately, after spending 50 days under "observation" at the McLean Hospital, traveled to Europe and attempted to gain status there as a refugee.

I later spent times of the order of five to eight months in hospitals in New Jersey, always on an involuntary basis and always attempting a legal argument for release.

And it did happen that when I had been long enough hospitalized that I would finally renounce my delusional hypotheses and revert to thinking of myself as a human of more conventional circumstances and return to mathematical research. In these interludes of, as it were, enforced rationality, I did succeed in doing some respectable mathematical research. Thus there came about the research for "Le Probleme de Cauchy pour les Equations Differentielles d'un Fluide Generale"; the idea that Prof. Hironaka called "the Nash blowing-up transformation"; and those of "Arc Structure of Singularities" and "Analyticity of Solutions of Implicit Function Problems with Analytic Data".

But after my return to the dream-like delusional hypotheses in the later 60's I became a person of delusionally influenced thinking but of relatively moderate behavior and thus tended to avoid hospitalization and the direct attention of psychiatrists.

Thus further time passed. Then gradually I began to intellectually reject some of the delusionally influenced lines of thinking which had been characteristic of my orientation. This

*began, most recognizably, with the rejection
of politically-oriented thinking as essentially a
hopeless waste of intellectual effort.*

*So at the present time I seem to be thinking
rationally again in the style that is characteristic
of scientists.*

The causes of the schizophrenia that so severely impacted
the life of John Nash are currently not well understood
by the scientific community. There may be both genetic
and environmental aspects to the onset of this disorder of
the mind. It has been observed that drugs that enhance
the formation of dopamine in the brain increase the
severity of schizophrenia symptoms which may suggest
that dopamine is in someway involved, but no one really
knows for sure at this point what the neurobiological
sources of this mind disorder are.

Have you heard of the "God Helmet"? Persinger has
conducted research aimed at determining if there are
two "selfs" associated with a human being, the first and
most dominant associated with the left-hemisphere of the
brain, and the second less dominant associated with the
right-hemisphere of the brain (10). To do this, he employed
what has been popularly known as the "God Helmet". This is
basically a football-type helmet that has electrical solenoids
mounted on its left and right hand sides to expose the left,
the right, or both hemispheres simultaneously to a very
low level magnetic field of about 1 micro-tesla.

Persinger studied 48 right-handed people with the "God
Helmet", 24 men and 24 women. The four conditions

investigated were a sham field (no applied magnetic field), a field applied only to the left hemisphere of the brain, a field applied only to the right hemisphere, and a field applied to both hemispheres simultaneously. The most interesting result obtained was the report by the subjects that they experienced a "sensed presence" in the room with them. This was reported most often when both hemispheres of the brain were subjected to the magnetic field and a little less often when only the right hemisphere was subjected to the field. There were significantly fewer reports of this "sensed presence" when no magnetic field was applied or when the field was applied to only the left hemisphere.

In a later paper, Persinger elaborated on these results (11). He suggested that the "sensed presence" was the left hemisphere's "self" recognizing the existence of the right hemisphere's "self", as a result of the suitable application of the magnetic fields of the "God Helmet". He also noted that a significantly higher proportion of women reported the "sensed presence" as compared to men. As one 21 year old female reported: *"I felt a presence behind me and then along the left side. When I tried to focus on the position, the presence moved. Every time I tried to sense where it was, it moved around. When it moved to the right side, I experienced a deep sense of security like I have not experienced before. I started to cry when I felt it slowly fade away (we had changed the field patterns)."*

I end this chapter with a discussion of the placebo effect in medicine. The placebo effect is an interaction between the mind and the body that was first brought to the forefront attention of the medical community by Beecher in 1955 (12). The word placebo has an interesting background.

It is a Latin word and derives from the following Vesper prayer said by Christian monks: "Placebo Domino in regione vivorum". This translates as "I shall be pleasing to the Lord in the land of the living" and, in this context, placebo means "I shall please".

A placebo is an inert substance that is administered to a percentage of patients in clinical trials of actual medicines to provide a baseline for any potential positive effects of the medicines. By inert it is meant that the placebo does not produce any physiological effects on the body whatsoever. Examples of some placebos are saline solutions, lactose, and starch, but there are many more possible placebos depending on the situation.

Say you wish to test the effectiveness of drug A for its relief of the symptoms of a particular medical condition. You start with a group of people who have the medical condition and then divide them into two groups. The first group receives the test medicine, while the second group is given a placebo. Such investigations are typically double-blind, where neither the patients nor the investigators know who received the actual drug and who received the placebo. This is the methodology used in all testing of new medicines today, but it was not the case before the medical community became aware of the significant effects that placebos can have on patient results.

In his landmark 1955 article, Beecher showed that in clinical trials on 1082 patients for severe post-operative wound pain, doses of an inert placebo administered to patients produced a significant improvement in their symptoms, typically in about 35% of the patients who received the placebo. Placebos also have significant positive effects on disorders of autonomic sensation such as nausea, psychoneuroses, phobias, and depression, and disorders of factors under neurohumoral control, such as blood pressure and bronchial airflow. However, placebos have not been observed to be effective for all medical conditions. The placebo effect appears to be independent of gender, age, and intellectual level

How does the placebo effect work? Because there is no physiological process operative here, the conjecture is that factors in the brain are responsible for the mitigation of patient symptoms. Beauregard has reviewed brain neuroimaging studies of placebo effects in patients with Parkinson's disease (13). These studies have shown that a clinical placebo response is associated with the release of dopamine in the striatum, as well as reduced activity of single neurons in that area of the brain. However, the placebo associations observed in the brain are very far from a complete explanation of what actually produces the placebo effect on human medical conditions.

The discussions in this chapter should make it clear that our understanding of what makes up conscious reality is very far from complete. The fact is that we do not know how the inputs from our senses are actually compiled in the brain to generate what we perceive as waking consciousness. And there are many aspects of brain phenomena that are essentially uncharted at the present time. As the philosopher Immanuel Kant pointed out long ago, we can consciously perceive the phenomenon—the thing as it appears to us, but we do not know the true nature of the noumenon—the thing as it really is.

Unconscious Reality

The weather was perfect, the winds were favorable, and he and his catamaran slipped along effortlessly through the calm waters as he drank in the beauty of sea and sky. It doesn't get any better than this, he mused to himself in his solitude on the open ocean. But then things changed in an instant. Out of nowhere he saw an impossibly large wave approaching him rapidly. To his terror, the wave seemed to be nearly sixty feet high!

He had heard of rogue waves before, of course. He knew of a cruise ship that had been struck and nearly capsized a few years ago by an eighty-footer. But that could never happen to him. It was too rare an occurrence. And yet here was the reality of it very fast approaching. He tried desperately to steer his boat into the wave in an attempt to ride over it, but there wasn't enough time. He remembered the wave hitting him and being underwater for what seemed like an eternity while he desperately clawed at the water to get to the surface before his breath ran out. And mercifully he did, coming up alongside his now disabled and slowly sinking craft. Dragging himself onto the boat, he found his emergency dingy and pulled the cord to inflate it. Then he jumped into the raft and paddled out away from his boat, spending the next few minutes watching it sink beneath the now calm waves.

So now here he was, a wet, disheveled, and forlorn figure on a raft. The sea and sky looked the same but now they had a much more ominous feel. As he looked around, there was nothing but himself and his raft floating in solitude over the vast, flat, expansive desert of ocean. Try to stay calm, he thought, at least you're still alive. Be rational, assess your situation. So he tried. What did he have for survival? Well, there was one smallish paddle, but that was better than none. His eyes searched for the raft's emergency kit and it was thankfully still there. With shaking hands, he opened it and saw that its contents were pitifully few. He found only a bailing cup, a crude fishing assembly, a quart of fresh water, and a few energy bars. By this time, dusk was approaching and he suddenly had an overwhelming sense of fatigue, mixed with equal doses of fear and despair. He dreaded the onset of darkness.

And then he woke up.

Isn't it strange how dreams can seem so real at the time you're dreaming. Then you awake and realize that none of it was real at all. For a short period of time, you may remember some of the major aspects about the dream that you just had, but later just about all of it is gone from your conscious memory.

Dreams are one element of the phenomenon we call sleep. Why do we sleep? That is a very good question. After all, sleep occupies about one-third of the time that we spend on this Earth. It's one-third of our physical reality.

From an evolutionary viewpoint, there would seem to be no advantage to sleep; during sleep we are much more vulnerable to predators than when we are awake. Yet all animals require sleep for their survival. Most, like humans, sleep during the night. But there are nocturnal animals who sleep during the day and hunt at night.

Most humans need about eight hours of sleep per night to function optimally when they are awake. But the amount of sleep required can vary widely between individuals. Some relatively rare individuals only require 1-2 hours of sleep per night and can function just fine during their 22-23 waking hours. These lucky people can accomplish so much more and effectively have a much longer productive lifespan than the rest of us. Why is this?

The fact is that for most of us, sleep deprivation produces significant problems for humans. If we can't or aren't allowed to sleep for an extended period of time, our thinking processes become degraded and our physical functioning is severely impaired. Extended sleep deprivation can lead to mental illness and in the most extreme cases even death.

So clearly, sleep has a very important biological function. But what is it? The reality is that the exact function of sleep has not yet been positively identified by biological scientists. There are, however, four main theories. The first is that sleep allows the body to repair cells that have become damaged by metabolic free radicals. During the day when the metabolism is faster, more free radicals are produced. At night, the metabolism slows and the body has a chance to rid itself of excess free radicals. A second theory is that sleep helps us replenish the body's fuel, such as the molecule ATP that is burned when we are awake. A third theory postulates that sleep allows the brain to clean out superfluous synapses in order to make room for the new information that you have acquired during the day. And the final theory suggests that sleep allows your brain to replay the events of the day, thus reinforcing memory and learning. The need for sleep could be some combination of all four of these theories, or perhaps it is related to something else entirely. No one really knows. When William Dement, the founder of the Stanford University Sleep Research Center, was asked why we need to sleep he was quoted as saying: *"As far as I know, the only reason we need sleep that is really, really solid is because we get sleepy"*.

However, we do know that there are various stages of sleep. Research has determined that there are five sleep stages which take place in cyclic fashion during the night. Sleep begins with stage 1 sleep. In stage 1, you have moved into a light sleep phase where you can drift in and out of sleep, and where you can be awakened easily. Some people may experience a sense of falling and sudden muscle contractions during stage 1. Then you transition into stage 2, a somewhat deeper sleep level where eye movement ceases. Stage 3 constitutes an even deeper sleep level still, and finally stage 4 is considered to be the deepest level of sleep that can be attained. Stages 1-4 are referred to as NREM (non-REM) sleep. After stage 4, you rapidly move to the REM sleep stage, where REM stands for Rapid Eye Movement. It is in the REM stage that you experience your most vivid and memorable dreams. During REM sleep, your body is actually paralyzed to some degree so that you do not physically act out scenes from you dreams, which has the potential for self-injury to either you or your sleeping partner or both. A typical sleep cycle lasts 90-110 minutes on average, so you cycle from stage 1 to REM sleep a number of times during the course of the night. Typically, cycling from stage 4 sleep to REM sleep occurs only during the first couple of cycles. After that, the cycling is from stage 2 to REM.

For a young adult who has a conventional sleep-wake schedule and who is without any sleep complaints, the following is the general nature of a night's sleep:

- Sleep is entered through NREM sleep.
- NREM sleep and REM sleep alternate with a period of about 90 minutes.
- Slow wave sleep predominates in the first third of the night and is linked to the initiation of sleep.
- REM sleep predominates in the last third of the night and is linked to the circadian rhythm of body temperature.
- Wakefulness in sleep usually accounts for less than 5% of the night.
- Stage 1 sleep generally constitutes 2% to 5% of sleep.
- Stage 2 sleep generally constitutes 45% to 55%.
- Stage 3 sleep generally constitutes 3% to 8%.
- Stage 4 sleep generally constitutes 10% to 15%.
- NREM sleep, which comprises Stages 1-4, is typically 75% to 80% of the total night's sleep.
- REM sleep usually accounts for 20% to 25% of a total night's sleep.

The percentages of the various stages of sleep are a function of a person's age. Young children spend more of their sleep in NREM sleep than do older adults.

The various stages of sleep are largely characterized through the use of brain wave monitoring techniques. Brain waves are electrical signals emanating from collections of neurons in your brain. Neurons are specialized brain cells that transmit information by the transfer of electrical signals through the matrix of neuronal connections. The average human brain contains about 100 billion neurons and each neuron is connected to a number of other neurons via electrical connections called synapses. There are about 100 trillion synapses in the brain. Electrical voltages are generated along neuronal paths and across neuronal synapses by the flow of electrically charged ions such as sodium, potassium, chloride, and calcium in the brain fluid. The synapses are considered to be the critical path elements in the transfer of information throughout the brain.

Brain waves are measured by the technique called electroencephalography, EEG for short. In EEG, an array of electrical detection electrodes are attached to the scalp at various and numerous locations around the head. The EEG probes do not pick up the signals from individual neurons in the brain since these are much too weak. Rather, each probe picks up the signals from a large number of neurons in the general vicinity of the probe location. Thus, the probe signal is the summation of the individual voltage signals of very large numbers of neurons. These average electrical voltage signals vary with time in a wavy sort of pattern, and hence the name brain waves.

In the waking state, brain waves are of the beta type. Beta waves have a frequency of 15-50 Hz and an amplitude of less than 50 microvolts. In stage 1 sleep, the brain waves change to a combination of alpha waves (8-12 Hz frequency, 50 microvolt amplitude) and theta wave (4-8 Hz, 50-100 microvolts). Stage 2 sleep brain waves are of a spindle configuration (4-15 Hz, 50-150 microvolts) which essentially represents a bundled wave configuration, as well as so-called K-complex waves, which exhibit a distinct high-low microvolt configuration. In stage 3, the wave behavior is a combination of spindle waves and the onset of slow delta waves (0.5-2 Hz, 100-200 microvolts). And in stage 4, the deepest sleep level, the wave pattern becomes totally delta waves. After the end of stage 4, the brain wave pattern changes rapidly to the REM pattern associated with dreaming. REM waves are 15-30 Hz and less than 50 microvolts, and are thus similar to the waking brain wave pattern, except that the person is still asleep and dreaming.

Why do we dream? As with the question of "why do we sleep", there is no definitive answer at present. Sigmund Freud thought dreams were a manifestation of suppressed desires in our subconscious mind. However, this explanation has fallen out of vogue in recent times in favor of more brain-oriented interpretations. The activation-synthesis hypothesis suggests that the source of dreams lies in the brain stem, which then activates the mid and forebrain cortical structures. Another theory suggests that dreams are related to the processing of long-term memories, while still another theory posits that dreams are related to the removal of sensory impressions and ideas that were not fully developed during the waking state.

We may not know why we dream, but we certainly know things about the nature of our dreams. Here is what I know from my first-hand dreaming experience. I know that when I am dreaming, the dream experience seems just as real as the waking experience. I know that I am usually the primary character in the dreams I dream. I know that significant elements of my dreams are associated with my waking long term memories. I know that many of the narrative aspects of my dreams do not make logical sense, yet I accept these illogical aspects without question. I know that there is usually a tension in my dreams; I need to get somewhere or do something or achieve some goal. Sometimes there is fear in them. Never are my dreams of a calm nature. There is always some form of action. On rare occasion, I have moved my physical limbs in association with physical actions taken in the dream state (e.g. moved my arms and legs in a violent manner). There are people who I know in my dreams, but there are also characters who I do not know at all. I know that I dream in color. I know that when I awaken, I can only remember the most striking elements of my dreams, and then only for a short time. And finally, I know that I have never experienced waking lucidity while I am in my dreams.

But some people do experience lucid dreams. Basically, a person has a lucid dream when the person becomes consciously aware that they are actually dreaming while they are in the dream state. Robert Waggoner, an accomplished lucid dreamer, has written an interesting book about his lucid dreaming experiences (14).

Waggoner says that he first began having lucid dreams at age sixteen when he discovered a technique to induce the lucid dream state. The technique described is remarkably simple. Before you go to sleep, have the conscious thought that when you look at your hands while in the dream state, you will become lucid and aware that you are dreaming. This was the technique Waggoner employed to induce his first lucid dream, as he described below (14):

> *I'm walking in the busy hallways of my high school at the junction of B and C halls. As I prepare to push the door open, my hands spontaneously fly up in front of my face! They literally pop up in front of me! I stare in wonder at them. Suddenly, I consciously realize, "My hands! This is a dream! I'm dreaming this!" I look around me, amazed that I am aware within a dream. All around me is the dream. Incredible! Everything looks so vivid and real.*

The experimental breakthrough in lucid dreaming took place when people discovered that the rapid eye movements in REM could be used to communicate to a researcher that the dreamer had achieved the lucid state. Prior to dreaming, the dreamer was instructed to move his eyes from left-to-right and back again a distinct number of times in succession. This would let the researcher know that he was indeed lucid. A brilliantly simple technique! Using this method, research has shown that the time frame during dreaming is the same as the time frame during waking. A five minute dream sequence takes five minutes in real time.

One of the interesting things lucid dreamers report is false awakenings; that is, they wake up from their dream only to realize that they are now in another dream. This can be quite disconcerting. Robert Waggoner reported this had happened to him a total of seven times during one overall dream state (14):

> On a beautiful summer morning I had an enjoyable lucid dream and woke from it, only to notice a different nightstand. Oh! A false awakening. But that was just number one. The first two didn't bother me, but then came three and four! Each time, I expected to find my real room, my real bed, but I kept finding very similar realities, close models of my bedroom. Then five, then six! Six false awakenings! My god, what was happening? Where was my world? It felt as if I was bursting through layers of probable worlds as the layers kept giving way! At that final, apparent awakening, my mind swirled in a whirlpool of memories, perceptions, realizations, and ephemera, grasping for an actual actuality! Finally, I slipped out of bed, steadied myself, and touched the light-blue plaster wall, hoping for nothing more than precious stability. After seven, I told myself that whatever reality I might encounter in the hallway, I would accept—that's how shaken I was—any reality was fine, as long as it stayed put.

Another intriguing aspect Waggoner came to realize through experiencing many, many lucid dreams was that he was not in total control of his dreams. He detected that there were dream characters who seemed to be acting under a volition that was not his own. Eventually, he came to the conclusion that the real controlling factor in his dreams was a much larger condition of "awareness" that transcended his sense of self.

Waggoner described evolving through five different stages of lucid dreaming as a result of his lucid dream experiences. Stage 1, the initial stage, revolves around personal play, pleasure, and pain avoidance. The dreamer feels that the dream only reflects him and his personal realm. Dream behavior involves the pursuit of play and pleasure and dealing with various attractions and distractions that may occur. The goal of the dreamer is to maintain the lucidity of the dream. He also experiences fearful situations that he cannot control, and tries to minimize any painful dream trauma.

Stage 2 of lucid dreaming involves an active attempt to manipulate movement by the dreamer. He may try to change the objects in the dream to meet his desires and objectives, and to experiment with the limits of his active control of the dream environment. In Stage 2, the lucid dreamer may experience false awakenings.

In Stage 3, the lucid dreamer actively begins experimentation with the dream environment and the organizational direction of the dream. He attempts to control the dream with his thoughts. However, he also notices that unexpected events occur in the dream that he did not have any intent to be present. The dreamer starts to have the feeling that there are "independent agents" who are active in his lucid dream.

Stage 4 leads the dreamer to try and explore the nature of the "other" that seems to be present in the dream and in control of aspects of the dream. The dreamer begins to develop a realization that the dream itself constitutes another level of reality that was previously unknown to him.

Finally, in Stage 5 the lucid dreamer develops a metaphysical connection with a larger level of awareness. The nature of this larger awareness is not clear; it may be his subconscious mind or perhaps some higher reality. The dreamer feels that everything exists as a part of a larger, interconnected oneness.

In the first three Stages of lucid dreaming, the dreamer makes the assumption that "I am dreaming this". However, in Stage 4 the dreamer realizes that the dream is not totally created by him, but is rather co-created by him and an "other". In Stage 5, the dreamer moves into a state of expanded awareness. Robert Waggoner's lucid dream experiences have convinced him that the waking self may be only a small portion of the totality of awareness.

The dreaming REM state takes up a portion of the sleep state, but the larger portion involves non-REM conditions. What is taking place during non-REM (NREM) sleep? This is an important question for which there are relatively few answers at present.

The fact is that we enter into the state of sleep each night via NREM rather than REM sleep. I have actively tried to see if I can consciously detect the beginnings of my nightly sleep. I am consciously awake and concentrating on trying to stay awake, but then I am not. It seems as though a veil suddenly drops depriving me of my conscious awareness. No matter what I do or how hard I concentrate, I cannot stop this veil of sleep from dropping. It's rather disappointing actually.

Researchers are starting to probe the boundary between wakefulness and sleep, and in particular why we lose waking consciousness when we drift to sleep each night. In one such study, a specific region of the brain known to receive motor signals and then transfer them to another brain location during waking states was stimulated using an electromagnetic pulse (15). This stimulation pulse did not change the brain wave patterns during both the waking and the NREM states, indicating no effect of the pulse on the waking or the sleep state. There was, however, a marked difference in the evoked electrical potential measured at the specific brain location that was targeted. During wakefulness, the pulse excited this brain area immediately and then the brain area continued to be active with further time. However, during NREM, while the pulse also initially activated the brain area, the initial activation rapidly died out. Thus, there was a significant difference between waking and NREM on the operation of the specific brain area. The researchers suggested that this was related to a loss of consciousness, due to a loss of "connectivity" in the brain cortical region during NREM sleep.

What can we say about the mental processes that may (or may not) occur during NREM sleep? The thing that distinguishes NREM sleep from REM sleep is the lack of rapid eye movements. These rapid eye movements have been associated with the process of dreaming that occurs extensively in REM sleep. But is there any mentative dreaming during NREM sleep?

Studies have indicated that there is some level of cognitive activity happening during NREM sleep. This cognitive activity is displayed when a person is awakened from NREM sleep and reports what they were experiencing. Here is the report of a person who was awakened from NREM sleep by two blasts of a 500 Hz tone (16):

> *a little whistling tone was going on . . . and then it went off. And (the other person) said 'Oh, you had better get things over with quickly, because you may have to wake up soon' . . . I just said 'Oh!' to this, and I think I heard the whistling noise again. Then the same scene was there for some time, and I was just walking around trying to think of what was going on.*

This account suggests the person was having some sort of dream experience during NREM sleep. However, the recall of dream-like experiences is significantly less for NREM as compared to REM sleep. It should be noted that in many cases there is no cognitive recall at all upon being wakened from NREM. Phenomena such as sleepwalking, sleeptalking, and night terrors have been reported during NREM sleep.

Investigations have been conducted to compare effects of REM sleep depravation to NREM sleep depravation. Disruption of REM, but not NREM, sleep diminishes the performance on basic visual discrimination tasks and on procedural or implicit memory tasks. Furthermore, the waking recall of stimuli presented during sleep is superior for stimuli that are presented just before awakenings from REM sleep as compared to NREM. It has been observed that evoked potentials longer than about 100 milliseconds are significantly diminished in NREM as compared to REM sleep. Short term memory is better after REM sleep awakenings as compared to the NREM case. Stories related after REM awakenings are more "dreamlike" than those related after NREM waking, and words reporting visual imagery are more prominent in REM as compared to NREM accounts. Finally, PET brain imaging studies have shown more widespread brain activity in REM sleep than in NREM sleep.

Do we do some diminished level of dreaming during NREM sleep? Studies suggest that some amount of cognitive activity is going on, but it is not clear that REM-type dreams are taking place during the NREM sleep state. However, it does seem clear that something is occurring within the brain during the NREM state.

I have had one experience that may relate to this question. I was on travel and asleep in a hotel in a distant city somewhere. I seemed to be sound asleep and not dreaming at all, when all of a sudden I heard a distinct "shout" in my mind. It seemed like a person had just made a loud shout in my hotel room. Upon hearing this, I became instantly awake! This was no groggy awakening. One second I was asleep and the next second I was wide awake with all of my cognitive faculties operating at full capacity. Upon this dramatic and sudden awakening, I listened intently to determine if I could hear any other noise in the hotel room but there was nothing, it was completely silent. This event impressed me enough that I still remember it vividly, which is why I include it here. Who or what was the source of the distinct shout that woke me that night? I still do not know. One thing I do know—it was not a dream.

It is worthwhile to consider two unusual aspects of sleep behavior. The first is sleepwalking and the second are people who require very little sleep for optimum waking functioning, so-called "short sleepers".

Sleepwalking typically happens during NREM sleep and is not associated with dreaming. The sleepwalking behavior of a man prone to sleepwalking was studied and here is a description of his sleepwalking state (17):

> During a second polysomnographic recording the following night, an episode of sleepwalking was seen during slow-wave sleep. The patient stood up with his eyes open and a scared facial expression. After a few seconds, he sat down, pulled on the EEG leads and spoke a few unintelligible words. The EEG showed diffuse, high-voltage rhythmic delta activity.

Clearly, the sleepwalker was in deep NREM sleep since he displayed a rhythmic delta brain wave activity during his sleepwalking episode. Also very interesting is the fact that his eyes were open during the sleepwalk, and that he spoke some unintelligible words. Using brain blood flow monitoring methods, the researchers observed decreased blood flow in the frontoparietal cortices of his brain during the sleepwalk, which is consistent with NREM sleep and the associated fact that sleepwalkers do not remember any of the details of their sleepwalk. So the basic question is: Who was doing the walking, seeing, and talking here?

A "short sleeper" is a person who needs only four hours or so of sleep a night to function during the day quite regularly, effectively, and happily. Such people constitute about 3% of the overall population. They are typically people who are energetic, positive in attitude, high achievers, and relatively thin. Their limited sleeping time occurs quite naturally and they do not sleep longer periods of time on the weekends. They also do not need naps during the day or coffee as a stimulant. This short sleep behavior begins in their childhood. The short sleeper feels very alert and refreshed upon awakening, even though they have had only half of the sleep that is normally required by most people. Studies have shown that short sleeping behavior is a genetically inherited trait. It cannot be developed by normal sleepers and attempts to do so only result in sleep deprivation. However, there is no current understanding about the brain mechanisms that lead to short sleep characteristics. So short sleepers are blessed. They have significantly more waking life than the rest of us.

The next brain-consciousness subject I would like to discuss is anesthesiology. Like sleep, anesthesiology can cause one to lose consciousness. I have been anesthesized only twice in my life thus far. The first time was when I was a child of five and had to have my tonsils removed. I have a vague memory of a mask being placed over my nose and mouth and a funny smell. The funny smell was probably ether or chloroform.

The second time I was anesthesized was when I needed a colonoscopy done at age 57. They had me disrobe and put on one of those awkward hospital gowns. Then they told me to lay on a gurney and the anesthesiologist inserted a needle into one of the veins of my arm. As he was pumping the anesthetic into my vein, he said he would start counting down from the number ten and that I would be out cold before he got to zero. So he began counting (I was concentrating to stay conscious as long as I could) but by the time he got to the number six, I was unconscious and never did hear him call out the number five. I don't remember having any dreams while under anesthesia for the colonoscopy. I just woke up and the whole thing was thankfully over.

The methods of anesthesia have developed dramatically over the past two hundred years. In the early 1800's, opium and alcohol were all that were available to ease patient suffering during extremely painful operations such as removing limbs. Unfortunately, these treatments were less than fully effective for pain, and the "medications" had significant issues with addiction. But better something than nothing from the patient's viewpoint.

Rather interestingly, ether was first discovered in the year 1275 by the alchemist Ramon Llull, which he called "sweet vitriol" (it was not given the name ether until 1730). In 1772, Joseph Priestley discovered nitrous oxide and it was developed by Humphry Davy. It was Davy who coined the name "laughing gas" since laughing was one of its side effects when it was inhaled. Both ether and nitrous oxide were not initially employed as anesthetics, but rather as recreational drugs of the early 1800's. People back then were known to have parties where they got "high" on ether and nitrous oxide. Who would think that the people way back then presaged the decade of the 1960's.

The discovery of gaseous anesthesia is credited to a group of three men. Crawford Long, a small town physician in

Georgia, claimed that he had first used ether for surgery in 1842. In 1844, the dentist Horace Wells revealed that he had used nitrous oxide for dental procedures, but his public demonstration was unfortunately only partially successful. In 1845, William Thomas Morton demonstrated the effective use of ether for general surgery at the Massachusetts General Hospital in Boston. It was Morton's demonstration that led to general acceptance of gaseous anesthetics by the medical community. In about 1848, James Simpson in England discovered the anesthetic effect of chloroform. This was much publicized when Queen Victoria used it in 1853 for the birth of her son Leopold. It wasn't until the 1900's that injectable anesthetics were developed. This began in 1934 with the discovery of sodium thiopental and since that time a host of injectable anesthetic drugs have been discovered. Modern intravenous anesthetics for surgery include barbiturates, propofol, etomidate, and ketamine, while inhalatinal anesthetics are nitrous oxide, isoflurane, sevofluorane, and desflurane.

The interesting thing about general anesthetics is that they totally suppress waking consciousness through chemical effects on the brain. How does this happen? An answer to this question could shed significant light on the nature of waking consciousness. The current concept is that anesthetics affect the ion channels that regulate synaptic transmission and membrane potentials in key regions of the brain (18). These effects then produce a brain state similar to NREM sleep. Anesthetic-induced unconsciousness is often associated with a deactivation of certain brain areas such as the thalamus, mesial parietal cortex, posterior cingulate cortex, and precuneus. But research has begun to suggest that, as is the case with sleep, unconsciousness results not from deactivation but from a disruption of cortical connectivity in the brain (15). However, the detailed aspects of such brain connectivity disruptions are presently unknown. So basically we know that anesthetics suppress waking consciousness, but we don't know precisely how.

I now turn our attention to the subject of hypnosis and its effect on the brain and consciousness. Hypnosis has been around as a practice since the 19th century. Today, it is an established medical procedure for dealing with psychiatric, pain, and habit disorders. Yet the scientific and medical communities have relatively little real understanding of the nature of the hypnotic state.

The Webster's dictionary definition of hypnosis is the following: *A trancelike state of altered consciousness that resembles sleep but is induced by a person whose suggestions are readily accepted by the subject.*

Based on brain wave measurements, it is certainly not a state of sleep. Under hypnosis, people can remember things they cannot recall in their conscious state. They can remember very specific details of events they have experienced, even many years after the fact. This aspect is sometimes used in the investigative work of criminal cases. While hypnotized, people can be made to perform physical feats they would normally find quite difficult or impossible to do in their conscious state, such as holding out their arms motionless for extended periods of time or immersing a hand in ice water for a long time. People can also be given post-hypnotic suggestions by the hypnotist, which they then proceed to follow once they are out of the hypnotic state.

Studies of hypnosis using experiential analyses have identified a series of aspects that characterize hypnotic states. These aspects include feelings of deep mental relaxation, mental absorption, a diminished tendency to judge and censor, a suspension of usual orientation toward time, location, and/or sense of self, and the experience of one's own response as automatic or extravolitional.

The hypnotic state is most often induced in a person by the actions of a hypnotist. Here is a typical example of a hypnotic induction from the Stanford Hypnotic Susceptibility Scale which is used to evaluate an individual's susceptibility to be hypnotized. The hypnotist is speaking to the subject (19):

> *Do you see the black pin up on the wall over there? I am going to refer to that pin as the "target". What I would like you to do is to relax in the chair, look steadily at the target, and listen to my voice.*
>
> *Please look steadily at the target and while staring at it keep listening to my words. You can become hypnotized if you are willing to do what I ask you to, and if you concentrate on the target and on what I say.*
>
> *Just do your best to concentrate on the target, to pay close attention to my words, and let*

happen whatever you feel is going to take place. Just let yourself go.

Now take it easy and just let yourself relax. Keep looking at the target as steadily as you can, thinking only of it and my words. If your eyes drift away, don't let that bother you . . . . Just focus again on the target.

Pay attention to how the target changes, how the shadows play around it, how it is sometimes fuzzy, sometimes clear. Whatever you see is all right. Just give way to whatever comes into your mind, but keep staring at the target a little longer.

After a while, however, you will have stared long enough, and your eyes will feel very tired, and you will wish strongly that they were closed. Then they will close, as if by themselves. When this happens, just let it happen.

You are comfortably relaxed, but you are going to relax much more, much more. Your eyes are now closed. Just keep your eyes closed until I ask you to open them or to wake up.

Now take it easy and just let yourself relax. Don't be tense. Just listen carefully to my voice. If your thoughts wander away from it, that is all right, but just bring your attention back to it. Sometimes my voice may seem to change a little, or sound as if it were coming from far off. That is all right. If you begin to get sleepier, that will be fine, too. Whatever happens, accept it, and just keep listening to my voice as you become more and more relaxed. More and more relaxed. Just listen and relax. Whatever you feel is happening, just let it happen.

Relax more and more. As you think of relaxing, your muscles will relax. Starting with your right foot, relax the muscles of your right leg . . . . Now the muscles of your left leg . . . . Just relax all over. Relax your right hand, your forearm, upper arm, and shoulder . . . . That's it . . . . Now your left hand . . . . And forearm . . . . And upper arm . . . . And shoulder . . . . Relax your neck, and chest . . . . More and more relaxed . . . . Completely relaxed . . . . Completely relaxed.

You are relaxed, very relaxed. By letting yourself go you can become even more relaxed. You can reach a state of deeper, more complete relaxation. You are becoming increasingly drowsy and sleepy. There is a pleasant feeling of numbness and heaviness throughout your body. You begin to feel so relaxed, so sleepy. It is easier to bring back your thoughts from other things and to attend only to my voice. Soon you will just listen sleepily to my voice, as you become more and more deeply relaxed.

You are relaxed, very relaxed. Your whole body feels heavy and relaxed. You feel a pleasant, warm tingling throughout your body as you get more and more tired and sleepy. Sleepy. Drowsy. Drowsy and sleepy. Keep your thoughts on what I am saying; listen to my voice. Soon there will be nothing to think of but my voice and my words, while you relax more and more. There are no troubles, no cares to bother you now. Nothing seems important but what my voice is saying, nothing else is important now. You are interested only in what my voice is saying to you. Even my voice may sound a little strange, as though it comes to you in a dream, as you sink deeper into this numbness, this heaviness, of deep relaxation. Relax, relax . . . . Deeply relaxed . . . . Deeper, deeper, and deeper.

Soon I shall begin to count from 1 to 20. As I count you will feel yourself going down, farther and farther, into a deep restful sleep, but you will still be able to do the sorts of things I ask you to do without waking up . . . . One . . . You are going to go more deeply asleep . . . . Two . . . Down, down into a deep, sound sleep . . . . Three, Four . . . More and more asleep . . . . Five, Six, Seven . . . You are sinking into a deep, deep sleep. Nothing will disturb you . . . . I would like you to hold your thoughts on my voice and those things I ask you to think of. You are finding it easy just to listen to the things I say to you . . . . Eight, Nine, Ten . . . Halfway there . . . . Always deeper asleep . . . .

Eleven, Twelve, Thirteen, Fourteen, Fifteen . . . Although deep asleep you can hear me clearly.

You will always hear me distinctly no matter how deeply asleep you feel you are. Sixteen, Seventeen, Eighteen . . . Deep asleep, fast asleep. Nothing will disturb you. You are going to experience many things I will ask you to experience . . . . Nineteen, Twenty . . . Deep asleep. You will not wake up until I ask you to do so. You will wish to sleep comfortably and to have the experiences I describe to you.

Now I want you to realize that you will be able to speak, to move, and even to open your eyes if I should ask you to do so, and still remain just as hypnotized as you are now. No matter what you do, you will remain hypnotized until I say otherwise.

The ability to enter the hypnotic state varies from person to person. Some people can be hypnotized quite easily, but some cannot be hypnotized at all. The reasons for this disparity are as unknown as the nature of the hypnotic state itself. Some hypnotists say that those who have practiced meditation over extended periods of time or those who can focus their minds on specific tasks are the types of people who can be hypnotized relatively easily. The Stanford Hypnotic Susceptibility Scale is composed of twelve tests of hypnotic suggestion. These twelve tests are: 1) Hand lowering (right hand); 2) Moving hands apart; 3) Mosquito hallucination; 4) Taste hallucination; 5) Arm rigidity (right arm); 6) Dream; 7) Age regression (school); 8) Arm immobilization; 9) Anosmia to ammonia; 10) Hallucinated voice; 11) Negative visual hallucination (three boxes); 12) Post-hypnotic amnesia.

Here is an example of the twelfth test for post-hynotic amnesia (19):

> *All right, now remain deeply relaxed but listen carefully to what I tell you next. In a little while I shall begin counting backwards from twenty to one. You will awaken gradually, but you will still be in your present state of hypnosis for most of the count. When I reach five you will open your eyes, but you will not be fully awake. When I get to one you will be entirely roused up, in your normal state of wakefulness.*

> *You will have been so relaxed, however, that you will have trouble remembering the things I have said to you and the things you did or experienced while you were hypnotized. It will prove to cost so much effort to remember that you will prefer not to try. It will be much easier just to forget everything until I tell you that you can remember. You will forget all that has happened until I say to you: "Now you can remember everything". You will not remember anything until then.*

> *After you open your eyes you may feel refreshed. I shall now count backwards from twenty, and at five you will open your eyes, but not be fully aroused until I say one. At one you will be awake . . . .*

> *A little later I shall take a pencil from the pencil holder on the desk. When I do so, you will get up from the chair you are in and move to the*

other empty chair in the room, and sit in it.
You will do this, but forget that I told you to
do so, just as you will forget the other things,
until I say to you, "Now you can remember
everything".

In the Stanford evaluation, a score of 1 is given for each of the 12 tests that are successfully completed by the subject. Thus, the range of possible scores is 0 to 12. People who cannot be hypnotized under any circumstances will get a score of 0. Those who have some possibility of being hypnotized will have scores in the range of 1-9, with a higher score indicating a greater propensity for hypnosis susceptibility. People who score in the range of 10-12 are considered to be "hypnotic virtuosos".

Significant research is being performed to determine the characteristics of brain function that are associated with the hypnotic state. Changes in brain waves occurring while in the hypnotic state have been investigated for a single hypnotic virtuoso subject who scored a value of 12 on the Stanford Hypnotic Susceptibility Test (20). The investigators observed that the state of hypnosis produced a re-organization in the composition of the subject's brain waves, particularly in the prefrontal and right occipital areas of the brain. The composition of the subject's brain waves also included spectral patterns during hypnosis that were completely different from those observed when the subject was not hypnotized. The hypnotic state induced a greater intensity of brain waves in the right side of the brain as compared to the left side. These brain wave results revealed that hypnosis was not a form of sleep, but rather a state of alertness and heightened attention.

During the hypnotic state, monitored EEG recordings did not show any sign of sleep (e.g. spindles, K complexes). Instead, the waking alpha rhythm was fragmented and replaced by periods of slower theta rhythms. Oculograms showed the occurrence of slow, roving eye movements.

Studies of the functional neuroanatomy of hypnosis have produced some important observations (21,22). In these studies, brain function during the hypnotic state was monitored by determining the distribution of regional cerebral blood flow, which was taken as an index of local neuronal activity. Positron-emission tomography (PET) scans were employed to establish this.

The PET results revealed that during the hypnotic state there was a great deal of activity in the occipital, parietal, precentral, prefrontal, and cingulated cortices of the brain. They showed that the hypnotic state exhibits cerebral processes that are different from those of simple memory, and suggested that this state was related to the activation of sensory and motor areas of the brain, but without any actual external sensory inputs or movement responses. The researchers concluded that the hypnotic state was not one of sleep, nor was it related to schizophrenic hallucinations. They indicated that it was a particular cerebral waking state where the subject, while seemingly in a sleepy mode, experiences a vivid, coherent, memory-based mental imagery that pervades the person's consciousness.

Hypnosis has been used in combination with anesthetics for human surgeries (23). The documented use of hypnosis in association with surgeries dates back to the

19th century when surgeons Jules Cloquet, John Elliotson, and James Esdaile performed major surgical procedures using hypnosis as the only anesthetic. The reason that such surgeries could be performed is that hypnosis was observed to eliminate surgical pain. At the present time, hypnotic techniques in combination with conventional anesthetics are being increasingly employed by the medical community.

That hypnosis can alleviate pain is medically well-documented (24). The pain threshold associated with stimulation of the supraorbital nerve is significantly increased by hypnosis as compared to the threshold without hypnosis. Pain associated with immersion of a hand in ice water is also significantly reduced, as is pain produced by intracutaneous electrical stimulation of a finger. Reductions in pain as a result of hypnosis have been observed for cases of severe burns, dental work, cancer, amputations, childbirth, spinal cord injuries, arthritis, postsurgical pain, unanesthetized fracture reduction, low back pain, headaches, and a host of other clinical pain problems. Research indicates that hypnosis provides substantial pain reduction for 75% of the patients treated with hypnotic techniques.

An interesting study has been conducted on pain that was not produced by an injury or stimulus, but actually induced only by hypnotic suggestion (25). Under hypnosis, the subject was given the hypnotic suggestion that pain was occurring, in the absence of any actual physically-induced pain. At the same time, the patient's brain was monitored with functional magnetic resonance imaging (fMRI) and it was observed that significant changes occurred in the brain areas of the thalamus, anterior cingulate, insula, prefrontal, and parietal cortices as a result of this hypnotically-induced pain. These are the brain areas that are also activated for real, physically-induced pain. There is clearly much to be learned about the state of consciousness produced by the brain configurations achieved as a result of hypnotic methodologies.

This chapter has attempted to summarize what we presently know about the nature of unconscious reality. It is not a great deal. The most we know about the transition from waking consciousness to sleeping unconsciousness is that it seems to involve an alteration in brain interconnectivity in some relatively vague way. To my mind, the lucid dreaming suggestions that REM dreams may contain larger elements of subconscious reality are thought-provoking, as is the non-REM character that comprises most of the sleep state, and the highly unusual nature of the hypnotic state. All of these aspects present a reality that we do not yet fully comprehend.

Scientific Reality

Science is the subset of philosophy that applies logic to experimental observations. The application of logic based on observations would seem to be a possible way to establish reality. This is essentially the scientific method. The 20th century saw the development of two major scientific paradigms that continue to shape scientific thinking about reality. These two paradigms are the theory of relativity and the theory of quantum mechanics. The first describes the behavior of the vast cosmos, while the second describes the behavior of the smallest pieces of matter and energy. We will now discuss each of these theories in more depth.

In the year 1905 Einstein published his famous theory of special relativity. It postulated a number of truly revolutionary concepts in physics. Prior to the publication of his theory, physicists conceived that there was a fixed, absolute frame of reference through which everything in the universe—the Earth, the Moon, the Planets, the Sun, the Milky Way galaxy—moved. Everything was contained in this three-dimensional framework, which was called the ether. Furthermore, light was a wave that propagated through the ether and the speed of light was dictated by the wave propagation velocity in the medium of the ether. This view implied that an observer's measurement of the speed of light should change depending on the direction it was measured with respect to the direction that the Earth was moving in the ether. Unfortunately, when scientists made such measurements, they observed that the speed of light was constant in every direction of measurement irregardless of the direction the Earth was moving in the postulated ether.

This was the quandary that physics found itself faced with in the year 1905 when Einstein published his revolutionary paper. What Einstein put forth was profound: No, there is no ether. Ether does not exist. Rather, the results of observations depend on the relative motions of the observer and the observed object. Furthermore, the speed of light is a constant of the universe. Nothing can travel faster than light; light is an absolute cosmic speed limit. Oh, and by the way it also predicted that matter was equivalent to energy, $E = mc^2$.

In 1916, Einstein published his general theory of relativity. This was a more general formalism than special relativity which incorporated the effects of gravity that influence cosmic bodies. Einstein's general theory said that, instead of three-dimensional space and independent time, the fabric of the universe was actually a four-dimensional spacetime. Large mass bodies in space had the effect of distorting spacetime and it was this distortion that produced the effects that we call gravity. Thus, matter traveling through space would be attracted to other pieces of matter as a result of this distortion. In effect, the gravitational field attraction between two objects of mass is really a distortion of spacetime. In addition, such effects also applied to electromagnetic waves such as light. Their travel through space would also be similarly affected. Einstein's general theory predicted that light rays could be "bent" when they traveled close to a large body in space such as a star.

Needless to say, Einstein's theory of relativity was so revolutionary that physicists at the time found it hard to accept as reality. However, in 1919 the astrophysicist Arthur Eddington traveled to Africa to study a total eclipse of the sun that could be observed there. What Eddington saw during the eclipse was that stars near the eclipsed disc of the sun appeared to be shifted in their positions. This meant the light from these stars was indeed being bent as it traveled near the sun, an observation that dramatically verified Einstein's prediction. As a consequence of this result, Einstein's theory of relativity became widely accepted by the scientific community.

Einstein's theory of relativity makes some rather startling predictions about the nature of reality. The first is that reality has a fundamentally relative nature. This means that what we observe depends on how we are moving in spacetime in relation to how the object we are observing is moving. One unusual aspect is called time dilation. This states that a clock on a spaceship traveling at a very high velocity relative to an observer who is stationary will move significantly slower than an identical clock in the observer's hand. According to the time dilation prediction of relativity, if one twin traveled close to the speed of light in a spaceship and then returned to Earth, he would discover that he had aged very little compared to his aged (or perhaps long dead) twin who had remained on the Earth. Quite strange, isn't it? But Einstein's prediction of time dilation has been confirmed by experiments comparing highly precise atomic clocks in orbit around the Earth to atomic clocks on the ground. An additional prediction is that a clock will run slower in a gravitational field as compared to one that is not in a gravitational field. Again, this has been verified experimentally. In fact, the GPS location system that is now in widespread use must correct for these relativistic time effects in order to make accurate location measurements on the Earth, due to the fact that the GPS satellites are moving at orbital velocity relative to the Earth.

Another prediction of Einstein's theory is that a moving object's length will appear shorter to an observer who is not moving relative to that object. This is called Lorentz contraction. Such an observed change in length only becomes appreciable at speeds close to the speed of light. For example, at a speed of 95,000,000 miles per hour (approximately 14% of the speed of light), the length of an object would decrease by only 1% as observed by the observer. However, at 90% of light speed, the observed object length would be 50% shorter than its stationary length.

A further prediction is that the observed mass of an object will increase as observed by an observer who is relatively stationary. This means that as an object moves faster and faster, its mass becomes greater and greater and it takes increasing amounts of energy to get the object to increase its speed. Since relativity theory predicts that the mass of an object becomes infinite at the speed of light, this dictates that no object can ever be accelerated to the speed of light, since this would require infinite energy. Indeed, such effects have been observed in ultra-high-energy particle accelerators here on Earth.

Einstein's theory also predicts that light will be observably bent when it travels in the vicinity of massive objects in space. As was mentioned, this was first verified experimentally by Eddington in 1919. However, a further ramification is that Einstein's theory predicts the existence and reality of "black holes". Black holes are objects in space where spacetime is so distorted (i.e. gravitational effects are so large) that nothing, not even light itself, can escape from them if it gets too close. Hence the reason why they are called "black". Black holes are postulated to form when large stars explode. Scientists now have a body of astronomical evidence that black holes indeed exist. In fact, there is thought to be a massive black hole at the center of our own Milky Way galaxy. The reason for this conjecture is because the stars at the galactic center move in very unusual orbits around an object that cannot be detected with our telescopes This object clearly has a massive gravitational field but it cannot be seen because it is dark and not emitting any electromagnetic radiation. Black holes are the true monsters of the universe. They are quite literally star and planet-eaters. Should a black hole come into the vicinity of our star and solar system, that would be the end of our local astronomical neighborhood and us in it.

Another reality aspect of black holes is the fact that at their center they are postulated to contain a "singularity", a mathematical point where spacetime and the laws of physics as we currently know them are changed radically. We will have more to say about the black hole singularity a bit later.

How did spacetime and the universe begin? The currently-accepted scientific theory is that the universe began approximately 13.7 billion years ago in a "Big Bang". Actually, the name Big Bang was a derogatory term coined by the famous astronomer Fred Hoyle, who espoused the opposing theory that the universe has always existed. It's interesting to note that the person who first formulated the Big Bang theory was a Belgium Catholic priest by the name of Father Georges Lemaitre. Lemaitre put forward the essence of the Big Bang theory in 1927, based on Einstein's general theory of relativity. The famous astronomer Edwin Hubble discovered experimentally that the distant galaxies in the sky were moving away from us, indicating that the universe was expanding. The discovery of the cosmic microwave background is also key to the foundations of the Big Bang theory, since this is thought to be the afterglow of that original stupendous event. At the very first infinitesimal fraction of a second of the Big Bang, all energy and all matter were contained within an infinitesimal volume of spacetime.

But there are two key questions about the Big Bang that scientists struggle with. The first is: What caused the Big Bang? And the second question is: Where was everything before the Big Bang happened? Some theorists have suggested that the Big Bang was produced by the point source collision of multi-dimensional "membranes".

The unfortunate thing about such theories is that they are impossible to prove or disprove by scientific experimentation, which puts them in the class of metaphysics rather than physics. As Terence McKenna nicely put it:

> *Modern science is based on the principle: "Give us one free miracle and we'll explain the rest". The one free miracle is the appearance of all the mass and energy in the universe and all the laws that govern it in a single instant from nothing.*

What is our universe made of? The present cosmological Standard Theory is that only 4% of the universe is composed of the matter and energy that we can presently detect! 26% of the universe is "Dark Matter" and the remaining 70% is "Dark Energy". An analogy for this is what a person sees when he (or she) looks at a sparsely populated mountainous region at night. You can see the pinpoints of light from the residences of the people who live there, but you cannot see the mountains.

Dark Matter, what is that? No one knows at present, but scientists say that we are all swimming in it. Dark Matter passes through your body all the time, but does not interact at all with the normal matter (i.e. matter composed of protons, neutrons, and electrons) that make up the atoms of your body. Science says that Dark Matter exists because of the gravitational effects that it has on ordinary matter. Our galaxy, the Milky Way, is encased in a sphere of Dark Matter. And so are all the other galaxies in the universe.

Even less is known about Dark Energy. Cosmologists describe the effects of Dark Energy as follows. If you have two volumes of space that are completely empty of matter, then these two volumes of empty space will repel each other, for reasons that are totally inexplicable at the present time. Essentially, these two volumes of space will exert a negative gravitational effect on each other. Science says that Dark Energy exists because there is no other way to explain the observational fact that the universe is continuing to accelerate in its expansion.

So at the present moment in time, science does not understand what makes up 96% of the universe! You cannot have a good handle on reality with such a limited amount of understanding.

Having summarized the current scientific understanding of the theory of relativity and the very large (i.e. the cosmos), let's now proceed to discuss the scientific understanding of the very small. Quantum mechanics is the field of science that deals with descriptions of the very tiny. It describes the behavior of sub-atomic particles, the electrons, protons, and neutrons that make up atoms, and the molecules made from atoms. It also describes the interactions of these species with electromagnetic radiation. Scientists consider quantum mechanics to be the basis for our understanding of how very small bits of matter and energy behave.

The roots of quantum mechanics go back to a concept put forward by Nobel Prize winner Max Planck in 1900 that electromagnetic radiation could be emitted by a heated body only with certain discrete energies that he termed "quanta". These discrete energies were the product of the frequency of the radiation multiplied by a term, h, which is now called "Planck's constant".

Quantum mechanics is based upon a famous equation called the Schroedinger wave equation. However Erwin Schroedinger, the scientist who formulated it, said that had he known to what use his equation would be put (namely as the basis for quantum mechanics), he would never have published it. Similarly, Einstein did not believe in quantum mechanics. His famous quote is that *"God does not play dice"*.

Why were Einstein and Schroedinger so adamantly opposed to quantum mechanics? Because it appears to strain scientific logic as we know it in all other aspects of science. The Nobel Prize winning "father" of quantum mechanics, Niels Bohr, famously said that anyone who wasn't disturbed by quantum mechanics doesn't understand it. Here are some examples that illustrate this conceptual difficulty.

In quantum mechanics, matter can behave either as a particle or as a wave, depending on the conditions of observation. This is called particle-wave duality. Let's consider the electron. If you have electrons running down a metallic wire, they act like individual particles. This is the basis of electricity. However, if electrons pass through a finely-spaced grating, they act like waves, forming interference patterns. This is the basis of the electron microscopes that are used to greatly magnify objects. So which is it? In the most fundamental sense, are electrons particles or are they waves? What is their inherent nature?

And why do they appear to behave differently based on the type of observation that is made.

The double-slit experiment was considered by Nobel Prize winning physicist Richard Feynman to be the best illustration of the particle-wave duality nature of quantum mechanics. The experiment is as follows. You have two fine parallel slits that electrons can pass through. On one side of these slits you have a source of electrons and on the other side a detection screen that tells you where an electron that passed through one of the two slits was located. Once an electron passes through a slit, it strikes the screen and leaves an image of where it struck. If the electron acts like a particle, then you will have only two slit-like images on the detection screen, since some of the electrons will pass through the left slit and some will pass through the right slit. That's what you would expect if the electrons behaved as only particles. However, this is not what you observe experimentally. Experimentally, you see more than just two slit-like images on the screen. What you see is an array of multiple parallel lines, with the intensity of the lines decreasing as you move away from the central two lines. This pattern is called a diffraction pattern and is characteristic of waves that are passing through a double-slit configuration. So what does the double-slit experiment tell you? First it tells you that the electron was a particle when it struck the detection screen. Second it tells you that the electron seemed to be a wave when it actually passed through the double-slits. Confusing, isn't it?

It gets weirder. If you put detectors at each of the two slits so that you can directly observe which slit an individual electron passes through, then the experimentally observed pattern is that of just two slit lines, as would be the case if electrons were particles. So if you don't make an observation of which slit the electron actually passes through, you get a wave pattern on the detection screen. But if you make an observation of which slit the electron passed through, then you get a particle pattern on the detection screen. Such experiments have conclusively shown that the type of observation you make determines what kind of electron reality you will observe. Reality is determined by the act of observation!

This type of particle-wave duality is not only observed for electrons, but also for photons, which are considered to be the "particles" that make up visible light and all other electromagnetic radiation. Experiments have also shown that carbon particles formed from 60 carbon atoms configured in the shape of a soccer ball (termed Buckminster fullerenes in the scientific literature) also show the particle-wave duality behavior.

The Schroedinger equation is the fundamental equation of quantum mechanics, which is used to describe the location and energy of particle-wave duality entities. This equation is based on a variable written as Ψ. Quantum mechanical solutions to the Schroedinger equation all occur as Ψ^2, which is taken to be the probability that a particle will occupy a given region of space. So Ψ^2 is a probability. But what is Ψ? Quantum mechanicists will tell you that Ψ is a "possibility wave". But that's not a very satisfying explanation because a "possibility wave" has no physical meaning. What the Schroedinger equation calculates is the probability that a particle will occupy a given region of space under the conditions that are specified at the start of the calculation. The Schroedinger equation constitutes the "mechanics" part of quantum mechanics. Quantum physicists plug in the experimental conditions, crank through the complex mathematics, and out pops a solution that can be observed by experiments. The major problem is that, until the act of observation is made, all the possible solutions of the Schroedinger equation are equally possible. The quantum mechanical terminology here is that the wave function calculated by the Schroedinger equation "collapses" to the observed solution as a result of the act of observation.

Erwin Schroedinger, the scientist who discovered the fundamental quantum mechanics equation that bears his name, put forward the following thought experiment to illustrate the difficulty that the act of observation plays in the reality described by quantum mechanics. It is called the "cat-in-the-box" experiment. A box contains a cat, along with a mechanical device that tracks the decay of a radioactive particle, which is a quantum event. If the radioactive particle decays, then the mechanical device releases a toxic gas that kills the cat. Now, before a person opens the box and takes a look (the act of observation), quantum mechanics says that the two states for the particle are equally possible, that is, the particle can decay or it does not decay. So then, logically, the cat is both dead and alive before the box is opened and the observation is made. That is the reality put forward by quantum mechanics.

Finally, consider quantum mechanical action-at-a-distance. Under certain conditions, two particles of light, two photons, can be emitted simultaneously from an atom, but traveling in opposite directions. Such photons are said to have quantum mechanical properties that are "entangled". Quantum mechanics predicts that by measuring a particular quantity of one of these so-called "entangled" photons, its polarization state, then the polarization state of the second photon is also determined. Effectively, the two photons are linked together even though they are physically separated. And it doesn't matter whether the two photons are separated by a fraction of an inch, one foot, 100 feet, 1 mile, 1000 miles, or 100,000 light years when you make your measurement on the first photon. The properties of the other photon are also instantaneously determined, even if the other photon may be across the galaxy! The physics community calls this phenomenon "nonlocality". The Irish physicist John Stewart Bell conceived of a way to experimentally measure photon entanglement and when the measurement was made in the 1980's, this prediction of quantum mechanics was actually observed to occur.

The experimental verification of nonlocality as a real physical phenomenon has very profound implications. Einstein deridingly termed this "spooky action-at-a-distance" and did not believe that it was possible because it takes place instantaneously (i.e. much, much, much faster than the speed of light) and does not involve the application of any physical forces that we know of. Yet, we now know that nonlocality is a phenomenon of nature.

So the three major mysterious aspects associated with quantum mechanics are: 1) particle-wave duality; 2) the role of the act of observation in creating reality; 3) nonlocality (spooky action at a distance). At the famous Solvay Conference in 1927, Albert Einstein and Erwin Schroedinger argued that the theoretical formalism of quantum mechanics was lacking in a foundation in physical reality. However, Niels Bohr and Werner Heisenberg won the day, and since that time quantum mechanics has been one of the two pillars of modern physics. The fact is that quantum phenomena are observed experimentally. Particle-wave duality is a reality of our universe. Spooky action at a distance (nonlocality) is a reality of our universe. These phenomena have been experimentally observed and established. How can the reality of these phenomena be explained?

What is the physics interpretation of reality associated with quantum mechanics? The one accepted by most physicists is the Copenhagen interpretation put forward by Niels Bohr in the 1920's (26). This interpretation divides things into two realms, the macroscopic and the microscopic. The macroscopic realm is that of our everyday experience and also that of our scientific measuring instruments. In this realm classical physics (i.e. the physics of Newton) applies. The microscopic realm is that of small things such as atoms and sub-atomic particles, where the Schroedinger equation describes the physics. The macroscopic instruments then make the observations that cause the wavefunctions of the microscopic world to coalesce into the observed state. Basically, this interpretation says, as the famous quantum physicist John Wheeler put it, that *"no microscopic property is a property until it is an observed property"*. In other words, the microscopic world has no intrinsic reality. Only that which is observed is real. Kind of hard-to-swallow, isn't it? But that is the essence of the

Copenhagen interpretation of quantum mechanics. Here is what Niels Bohr said:

> *There is no quantum world. There is only an abstract quantum description. It is wrong to think that the task of physics is to find out how nature is. Physics concerns what we can say about nature.*

The problem with the Copenhagen interpretation that observation creates microscopic reality is this: Who is the observer? Is the observer the piece of experimental equipment that makes the observation? The famous mathematician John von Neumann, in his 1932 comprehensive treatise on quantum mechanics "The Mathematical Foundations of Quantum Mechanics" (considered by many to be the "bible" of quantum mechanics), argued that no equipment could be the observer since any piece of experimental equipment can be considered as part of a larger quantum mechanical system. He argued that only a conscious observer could make the actual observation that collapsed the wavefunction to its observed value.

Another problem is that, while quantum phenomena clearly happen at very small scales of matter, when things get bigger the quantum nature disappears and things revert to the normal behavior that we see in our everyday lives. How the act of observation is associated with the transition from quantum scale effects to non-quantum classical effects is not at all clear. In other words, how does the larger environment act in some way as the observer?

Yes, the role of observation in creating the reality has given physicists major heartburn since the beginnings of quantum mechanics. In 1957, the physicist Hugh Everett put forward a concept called the "many worlds" interpretation that did away with the act of observation. The "many worlds" interpretation says that there is no observational collapse of the wavefunction. Instead, all the possible outcomes of the wavefunction occur in reality; it's just that each of them happens in a distinct, separate universe. So the act of observation is replaced by an infinite number of co-existing universes, the so-called "multiverse". Stated another way, there is no single reality but rather an infinite number of realities. Mindboggling, yet physicists are increasingly being attracted to the "many worlds" interpretation because of the difficulties associated with explaining how observation creates reality.

In summary, the quantum phenomena of particle-wave duality and nonlocality are firmly established by experimental physics. These phenomena are inextricably interwoven into the fabric of our physical existence. However, according to quantum mechanics the reality that forms the basis of these phenomena either does not exist (Copenhagen interpretation) or consists of an infinite number co-existing universes (many worlds interpretation). At its root, quantum mechanics seems like a bizarre dream.

Now let's discuss the stuff of the universe, matter and how matter interacts with the forces of nature.

Matter is what we interact with in the physical world every day of our lives. Our bodies are matter. The air we breathe,

the water we drink, and the food we eat are all made of matter. All of the possessions that we own are matter. Our homes, our cars, our furniture, our dishes, our TV set and computer, all matter. The Earth, the Moon, the Sun, the Planets are made of matter, as are all the other stars and planets in the vast universe. Matter is ubiquitous alright. But is there anything "the matter with matter"?

Physicists presently have what they call the Standard Model of matter. Start with a chuck of stuff, say a dinner spoon for example. The spoon is composed of individual atoms. There are a limited number of different types of atoms in our known universe, and each different atomic type is called a chemical element. Each individual atom is considered to be composed of a nucleus and surrounding orbital clouds of electrons. Because the nucleus is much smaller than the electron clouds, most of the atom is empty space, essentially a vacuum. Thus, atoms are mostly empty space!

The different atoms in our universe are represented by what is called the Periodic Table of the Elements. This table was discovered in 1869 by the Russian chemist Dmitri Mendeleev based on an ordering of the chemical properties of the different elements. The columns of the table contain elements that have similar chemical properties. The sequence of the elements in the periodic table is dictated by the atomic number of the element, which is the number of protons in the nucleus of that particular type of atom. Thus, hydrogen is the first element in the Periodic Table, with an atomic number of 1 since it has only one proton. Among some of elements commonly known to the general public, carbon has an atomic number of 6, nitrogen is 7, oxygen is 8, aluminum is 13, iron is 26, copper is 29, silver is 47, gold is 79, and uranium is 92. It should be noted that elements of higher and higher atomic number continue to be discovered. The current highest element has an atomic number of 118, and is called by the latin pronunciation of this number, ununoctium. The Periodic Table is essentially the chemist's starting point for investigating chemical reactions, since it also provides an ordering of the chemical bonding electrons of the various elements, as dictated by the fundamental theory of quantum mechanics.

In addition to the atomic number, each element has what is called an atomic weight. The atomic weight is essentially the sum of the weights of the protons and neutrons that make up the atomic nucleus (the weight of the electron is only 1/1836 of the weight of a proton or neutron and is thus negligible in comparison). The weight of a single proton (or neutron) has been measured to be 1.673×10^{-27} kilogram. Because the individual atoms of an element can have a different number of neutrons in the nucleus (i.e. different isotopes), the atomic weight of the element is given as the average over all the possible isotopes of that element.

So atoms are made up of protons, neutrons, and electrons. Electrons are fundamental particles, but not protons and neutrons. These are composed of smaller particles which are called quarks. This rather strange name was put forward by Nobel Prize winner Murray Gell-Man who found this unusual word in the book Finnegans Wake by James Joyce. According to the Standard Theory, protons are composed of two up-quarks and one down-quark, while neutrons are composed of one up-quark and two down-quarks. Don't ask what up-and down-mean. Another fundamental property is charge. Protons have a charge of +1, neutrons have zero charge, and electrons have a charge of -1. These particles also possess a fundamental property called "spin". One should not regard the particles as actually spinning. Rather, the property of spin derives from the theory of quantum mechanics. Electrons, protons, and neutrons all have a spin value of ½, for reasons that derive from quantum mechanics.

In addition to protons, neutrons, and electrons, there are other types of particles encountered in the Standard Theory. These include positrons (electrons with a charge of +1), anti-protons (protons with a change of -1), electron neutrinos (no charge and almost no mass), muons (a more heavy variant of the electron), muon neutrinos, tau particles (heavier than muons), and the tau neutrino (postulated but not yet discovered).

Positrons and anti-protons are termed anti-matter particles. Positrons and anti-protons have even been combined to synthesize anti-hydrogen atoms. While the amount of naturally-occurring anti-matter in our observable universe is almost vanishingly small, scientists surmise that there may be whole far-distant galaxies that are composed entirely of anti-matter. We should hope these hypothesized galaxies are very far away from us, for whenever an anti-matter particle encounters a matter particle, they immediately annihilate each other in a flash of blinding energy.

Neutrinos constitute an important class of sub-atomic particles because of the fact that there are so many of them in the universe (they are generated by reactions in stars). Most of the neutrinos that strike the Earth emanate from our Sun as a result of the nuclear reactions that occur there. Because neutrinos have no charge and a very, very, very small mass (thought to be less than one millionth of the electron mass) they exhibit almost no interactions with ordinary matter. In actual fact, about 65 billion neutrinos per second hit every inch of your body all the time, but essentially pass right through it without affecting your body in any way. In 2011, scientists reported a stunning experimental result that neutrinos appear to travel slightly faster than the speed of light. If this result is confirmed by further experimentation, it will seriously undermine the pillar of Einstein's theory of relativity that nothing can travel faster than light speed. Should this result be verified, there will be a substantial impact on our scientific views of reality. We shall see.

All the particles we have described thus far are called matter-particles. But there is also another class of particles called force-particles. In the Standard Model, these are the particles which transmit the four fundamental forces of nature. Photons are the force particles that transmit the electromagnetic force. Particles called gluons are the bearers of the strong nuclear force that holds the quarks together in protons and neutrons. So-called W and Z particles are the bearers of the weak nuclear force responsible for some forms of radioactivity. And gravitons are hypothetical particles that are thought to be the bearers of the gravitational force. All of these force particles have been determined experimentally, except for the gravitons. Despite decades of searching, experimental physicists have yet to detect a single graviton particle.

There is one more force particle that is postulated by the Standard Theory, but not yet experimentally detected. This entity is called the Higgs particle and is thought to transmit the fundamental quantity of mass to all the other matter particles. In the popular media, the Higgs particle is referred to as the "God particle", based on Nobel Prize winner Leon Lederman's book by the same name. Lederman has admitted that his actual name for the particle was the "goddamn particle" because it was so important to the Standard Theory but so difficult to observe. Perhaps the name was shortened by his book editors, a circumstance that may have made it even more controversial.

There is no question that proving or disproving the existence of the Higgs particle is of premier importance to particle physics. This in fact is the primary purpose of the multi-billion dollar Large Hadron Collider (LHC) in Geneva, Switzerland. If the experiments at the LHC do not produce any convincing evidence of the Higgs particle, then the entire framework of the Standard Theory of particle physics will come into question and it may have to be radically altered or even replaced by some other theoretical framework.

Thus, our present scientific understanding of the nature of matter hangs in the balance at the present moment. It's funny how our perception of reality can sometimes turn on a dime (or on an experiment in this case).

But there's more. Cosmologists have made the observation that dark matter accounts for 83% of the matter in the universe, whereas the ordinary matter that is described by the Standard Theory accounts for only 17%! In 1975, cosmologists discovered that the stars in spiral galaxies were orbiting the galactic center at velocities much higher than could be accounted for by the distribution of normal galactic matter. This led them to postulate that the spiral galaxies were enveloped in a sphere of another type of matter. It was called "dark" matter because it neither emits nor scatters electromagnetic radiation. Subsequent cosmological studies have shown that, in fact, all of the galaxies in the observable universe are encased in this strange, dark matter.

And what is dark matter? No one really knows at the moment. However, we do know that it flows through everything on the Earth, you and I included, every moment of every day. But because it is so different, it does not interact in any way we can yet detect with ordinary matter. Physicists are at the present moment conducting large-scale experiments in deep underground mines to try and detect some sort of dark matter interactions, but thus far have been unable to do so. Since its discovery in 1975, no one has yet to develop any experimental description of dark matter. They are a number of theoretical speculations for sure, but these are only speculations in the absence of experimental results.

So what is "the matter with matter"? What is the reality of matter? Science simply does not know at the present time. Furthermore, what does science really know about both the grand and the tiny in our universe? Very little really.

Finally we come to the holy grail of science, the Theory of Everything (TOE for short). At the present time there are two parallel theories that are intrinsically incompatible with each other. The first is general relativity which describes the very large bodies in the cosmos and their interactions through the action of gravity. The second is quantum mechanics that describes the observed behavior of very small things like atoms and sub-atomic particles. In almost all cases of the application of quantum mechanics to the material world, the force of gravity is neglected because it is so small in comparison to the electromagnetic force, and the strong and weak nuclear forces. But there is one area in the universe where this is not the case. That location is at the center of a black hole.

General relativity predicts that there is a singularity at the center of a black hole, a very small point-like region where gravity is so strong, the mass density is so high, and the fabric of spacetime is so warped that the theory of general relativity breaks down. Physicists absolutely detest singularities. So there must be some melding of general relativity and quantum mechanics that occurs at the center of a black hole. The two theories must be made to fit together there in order to have a Theory of Everything. But, try as they might, theoretical physicists have been unable to come up with any approach that can meld general relativity and quantum mechanics together.

There is an interesting book entitled "The Trouble with Physics" by Lee Smolin, a theoretical physicist at the Perimeter Institute for Theoretical Physics, that discusses this and other major issues of physics relating to reality (27). In his book, Smolin puts forward five "great problems in theoretical physics" at the present moment in time. Problem number 1 is how to combine general relativity and quantum mechanics into a Theory of Everything. Problem number 2 centers around the vagueness of the nature of reality and the observational nature of reality that are at the core of the Copenhagen interpretation of quantum mechanics. Problems 3 and 4 are associated with the issues that have been discussed related to the Standard Theory of particle physics. And Problem number 5 is how to explain dark matter and dark energy. Smolin has very nicely summarized the major reality issues that currently face science in his five Problems.

But there are still some additional science-reality concepts that need to be considered. The first of these is the seminal work of the theoretical physicist David Bohm. David Bohm was born in 1917 in Pennsylvania and died in 1992 in London. One might say that his experiences between these dates were quite unusual at the very least. After graduating from Penn State, Bohm went to Cal Tech in 1939 to work as a graduate student in theoretical physics under Robert Oppenheimer. While at Cal Tech, he became involved with a number of local political groups with so-called leftist leanings, such as the Young Communist League, the Campus Committee to Fight Conscription, and the Committee for Peace Mobilization.

When Oppenheimer went to Los Alamos to develop the atomic bomb, he tried to bring Bohm along but Bohm was rejected by General Leslie Groves, Oppenheimer's military partner, who had heard that Bohm was a communist. So Bohm remained at Cal Tech doing his Ph.D. research there, with Oppenheimer as his off-campus advisor. He completed his Ph.D. thesis work in 1943 but it turned out that its subject matter was of usefulness to the Manhattan

Project, and so all his thesis data were immediately classified. Since Bohm did not have a security clearance, he could no longer access the information that he himself had generated. One wonders if this has happened to any other Ph.D candidate, before or since. However, it all worked out for Bohm's degree because in the end Oppenheimer certified to Cal Tech that Bohm had actually performed the research successfully, and he was awarded his Ph.D.

Bohm eventually obtained a position at Princeton University as an assistant professor and became a protégé of Albert Einstein, who had earlier emigrated from Germany to Princeton. However, in 1949 Bohm ran afoul of the McCarthy era communist paranoia. He was called to testify before the House Un-American Activities Committee and refused to testify. He was subsequently arrested for his refusal, but was acquitted on any charges in 1951. However, as a result of all this, he was fired from his professorship at Princeton. Einstein tried to convince Princeton to hire him back once he was acquitted, but they did not do so. Subsequently Bohm left the U.S. for good, becoming an expatriate first in Brazil, then in Israel, and finally in England, where he lived until his death. How's that for an intermingling of science and politics!

David Bohm is best known for developing the Pilot Wave theory of quantum phenomena. This concept had been originally put forward by the Nobel laureate Louis de Broglie at the famous Solvay physics conference in 1927. de Broglie was the person who first proposed the concept of particle-wave duality which became a pillar of quantum mechanics. However, he believed that electrons and photons were actual physical particles and not creatures created by the act of observation, as conceptualized by Niels Bohr and Werner Heisenberg. So he formulated the theory that electrons and photons were guided in their behavior by a wave function called a Pilot Wave. It was the Pilot Wave that went through both slits in the double-slit experiment and its doing so guided the individual particle, which only went through one of the slits, to its eventual position that made up the diffraction pattern observed on the screen by a large number of particles passing through the double-slit. However, unfortunately, de Broglie's idea was not accepted at the Solvay conference and the quantum mechanics formalism of Niels Bohr became the accepted dogma of the physics community.

David Bohm developed de Broglie's idea in considerably more detail. By associating the Pilot Wave with a so-called "quantum potential", Bohm was able to show that this alternative theory to quantum mechanics could actually reproduce all of the results predicted by quantum mechanics. This included particle-wave duality as well as non-locality. However, importantly, it said that there was a true underlying physical reality, as opposed to the quantum mechanical theory which postulated that the act of observation determined reality. The de Broglie-Bohm theory as it became to be known thus did away with the act of observation by introducing a "quantum potential". The major problem was that the "quantum potential" had no obvious physical source. Bohm considered that it was related to hidden variables in a sub-quantum system. It was the work of Bohm that inspired physicist John Stewart Bell in 1964 to develop his theory which eventually established the reality of nonlocality in our universe.

In his later years, Bohm expanded his thoughts about reality to develop what he termed "undivided wholeness and the implicate order" (28). He did this in an attempt to circumvent the problems with trying to unify the existing theories of general relativity and quantum mechanics. Essentially, Bohm proposed what might be called a new reality paradigm.

He said that what general relativity and quantum mechanics have in common is "undivided wholeness". What this means is that the specifics of our reality are just a part of a higher reality where everything is innately connected to everything else on a very fundamental level. Bohm took this more encompassing reality to be of a higher dimensional nature. He further postulated that the reality described by our current physics (general relativity and quantum mechanics) is something that is contained within or enfolded into this higher reality. Bohm stated that the physical ordering that we observe is essentially an "implicate (enfolded) order" that comes out of the greater reality under certain conditions. What our current physics describes is "explicate order" in that each physical thing lies only in its specific region of space and time and outside the regions belonging to other physical things. This is the basis for Bohm's new paradigm of "wholeness and the implicate order".

Bohm's reality postulate of "undivided wholeness and the implicate order" sounds somewhat like Buddhist philosophy. However, Bohm put forward two specific scientific phenomena that can help in the understanding of what he proposed.

The first is a phenomenon that is observed with the viscous flow of fluids. Consider the experiment where you have two concentric (one inside the other) glass cylinders with a layer of a viscous clear liquid such as glycerine in between the two cylinders. A drop of black insoluble ink is then placed in the viscous liquid and the outer cylinder is turned very slowly so that there is no turbulent mixing of the liquid. What you will observe is that the initial spherical ink particle becomes drawn out into a finer and finer filament shape as the outer cylinder is rotated more and more, until eventually this filament becomes so fine in size that you can no longer see it. From the point of view of your vision, it has effectively disappeared into the liquid as a result of the outer cylinder rotation.

But here comes the really interesting part. If you now slowly rotate the outer cylinder in the opposite direction, the ink filament will eventually start appearing again, and with a suitable amount of counter-rotation, the spherical ink drop will be totally reconstituted. So the ink drop that disappeared into the liquid has now been resurrected. Remarkable! Yet, this is a real physical phenomenon that anyone can observe to happen with the right equipment.

Bohm took this experiment to be a way to see how explicate reality, the reality that we experience and that our current physics describes, can be enfolded into a higher reality and extricated from this higher reality under the proper set of conditions. In other words, the implicate order is more fundamental than the explicate order.

To illustrate "undivided wholeness", Bohm evoked the physical phenomenon of the hologram. You may have experienced viewing holograms, say on your credit card or in a magazine. What you see is an image that looks three-dimensional and that seems to change its orientation as you change your angle of view. The visual image that you perceive is that you are actually looking at a three-dimensional object even though you know that what you are looking at is on a two-dimensional surface.

How are holograms formed? This is how. You take a light source and split the light beam into two beams with a beam splitter such as a half-silvered mirror. One of the beams goes directly to a photographic plate. The other one is redirected to illuminate a three-dimensional object and the reflections of the beam off that object then go to the photographic plate. At the plate, the two beams combine together to generate an interference pattern. Now comes the unexpected part. When you illuminate the photographic plate that has this interference pattern on it, what your eye sees is a three-dimensional image of the object. The image that you see looks three-dimensional. Furthermore, it doesn't matter whether you shine light on a large part of the plate or on a small part of the plate, you still get the same three-dimensional object. In other words, the three-dimensional "wholeness" of the object is contained in the photographic plate which is of a different dimensionality, namely two-dimensional.

What Bohm proposed in his new paradigm is an undivided wholeness of the totality of existence that is present in a dimensionality different from our present physical three-dimensional reality. Our entire universe with its subatomic particles, atoms, molecules, inanimate objects, and life forms is fundamentally an undivided wholeness.

These "things" are basically only manifestations of the localized flow (termed holomovement by Bohm) of the wholeness. Finally, Bohm postulated that our consciousness is also an integral part of this undivided wholeness.

It is clear that David Bohm has presented a new way of thinking about reality. The eminent physicist proposed something that seems like metaphysics, but has its roots in both general relativity and quantum mechanics. It is definitely worthwhile giving this some deep thought and intuitive reflection.

While this has taken us a long way from the reality conceived by our current scientific paradigms, there is still one more road to explore. And that road is the possibility that what we perceive as reality is really a virtual reality.

Remember that earlier I described the virtual reality portrayed in the movie "The Matrix". What if our physical reality is really a super-super computer virtual reality designed, built, and operated by someone or something in another, more expansive dimensional realm. In other words, we might really be only computer characters in a vast "Sims" program. As disconcerting and possibly depressing as this might sound, the fact is that such an idea can account for a large number of the current difficulties with explaining the fundamentals of the physics in our physical world (29). Here are some examples.

Our physical world is thought to have been created in a "Big Bang" 13.7 billion years ago, where everything appeared from nothing and where time and space were created. But one could argue that a cosmic virtual reality could also come from nothing, when the virtual reality was booted up on the super-super higher dimensional computer.

Then there is the physical observation that energy comes in the form of little packets, or quanta, as originally observed by Max Planck. In the virtual reality, energy equates to information. Virtual matter is simply condensed information. And in the virtual world, information is in a digital form in our computers. The "quantum" of digital information is a "1" or a "0". So the virtual approach has no difficulty explaining the existence of quanta.

Take the speed of light. The speed of light is the maximum speed that anything can travel in our physical world. Why do we have such a speed limit and what determines the speed? The virtual explanation is that rates in the virtual world must necessarily have an absolute maximum, this maximum being the processing speed of the super-super computer.

We have shown that the phenomenon of nonlocality is a mystery of quantum mechanics, the spooky action at a distance. How is nonlocality possible in our physical world? After all, nonlocality is a connectivity that occurs instantaneously irregardless of the distance between the interconnected species. The virtual reason is that a computer processor is equidistant from the computer screen pixels, so that its effects are essentially nonlocal to the screen effects.

General relativity in our physical reality says that space becomes curved in the presence of massive bodies, and that lengths contract and time dilates noticeably as one approaches the speed of light. In a virtual reality, such effects are associated with overloads of the processor network, which causes processing outputs to change.

In our physical reality, energy is always conserved. In the virtual reality, information, which is the virtual equivalent of energy, is always conserved. If this were not the case in a virtual reality then that reality would become unstable.

Finally, consider a number of quantum mechanics observations. First, quantum events are essentially random events without a deterministic cause. This is accomplished in a virtual reality through the use of a random number generator. Then there is the Heisenberg Uncertainty Principle which says that one cannot know precisely certain coupled properties such as a particle's position and its momentum. The more precisely we know one, the less precisely we know the other. In the virtual reality, calculating one property of a self-registering interface may displace complementary information at that interface. All quantum objects in our physical reality are absolutely identical to each other; all electrons are identical to one another and all photons of the same energy are identical. In the virtual reality, every digital object that is created by the super-super computer software is identical to every other similar digital object. And finally, quantum events take place in discrete "jumps" which constitute state transitions at the quantum level. The digital processes in a virtual reality could easily simulate event continuity as a series of state transitions, just like the individual frames in a movie reel.

So there you have it. The full range of realities that science presently has on its table and a couple that might be considered somewhat outside the box of current scientific dogma. Which one feels right to your intuition?

Unexplained Reality

As he looked up, he could see the vast, near-vertical slab of rock reaching to the sky, and all of its four hundred-foot height was intimidating. He felt a transitory knot in his stomach, but only briefly. After all, he was an experienced free-style climber who had climbed many a vertical face such as this one alone and without any rope. There was no room for error, sure, but he wasn't planning to make any mistakes. He would take it one step at a time, and slow and easy. Just a piece of cake. He was lean and mean and ready to go. It's not that he had a death wish, it was just the exhilaration of the danger and the pitting of his skills and determination and will against that of the rock. It made him feel alive.

He found his first foot and hand hold and pulled himself up off the ground, hugging the rock face. The rock had many knobs and fissures that he could use. His hands were coated with gripping dust so that he could get a solid connection to each of the holds. Step with the right foot, stabilize with the left hand, and reach up with the right hand. Then do the same thing with the left foot. Over and over, up and up. His breathing was rapid and his heart was pounding, but his mind was focused on each small incremental action. Just make sure that each little step and reach was good and solid.

He was in the zone and doing fine. The ground was now about two hundred feet below him. That was a long way, but he had no fear. There was just the rock and the sun and the light breeze and him. Life was good, he was good.

Then it happened. His right hand reached for its next hold in a crevice, but when he pulled himself up, the rock fractured and the right side of his body waved precariously away from the rock face. He didn't panic, this had happened to him many times before. What he needed to do was to stabilize himself with his other three limbs until he could find another hold. But then to his astonishment his left hand hold gave way. Now he instantly knew there was no possibility of recovery. As he plummeted downward, he wondered if he would feel anything when he hit.

And then he woke up.

There are a number of phenomena that people report which seem perhaps too bizarre to be part of our physical reality, but the key question is: Are they really? These are extraordinary aspects such as near-death experiences, out-of-body experiences, ghostly apparitions, and extra-sensory perception. These phenomena are generally relegated to the genre of the paranormal. Our current science has no basis with which to explain such things and prefers to dismiss them completely. However, in our quest for reality, they also deserve to be seriously examined and considered. After all, many things that were considered paranormal five hundred years ago are now firmly entrenched in our scientific thinking. Let's begin our discussion with the near-death experience (abbreviated as NDE).

One might say that death is the ultimate reality of life. What happens when we die, and after? Do we simply cease to exist or does our essence continue on some different plane of reality? These are age old questions to be sure, but that doesn't make them any less important now.

I first became aware of near-death experiences when I read the book "Life After Life" by Raymond Moody (30). I found "Life After Life" to be a totally fascinating book. It presented very thought-provoking and unusual information that I had never known before. A typical near-death experience was described as follows. A person felt as though "they", that is their consciousness, had left their body and that "they" were observing the scene below, typically a hospital room, from a vantage point above, usually near the ceiling. They could see their body and the medical personnel who were attending it. After some time of this observation, they then found themselves moving through a dark tunnel, with the feeling that they were moving at great speed. There was a bright, white light at the end of the tunnel. When they reached the light, which was dazzlingly brilliant, they experienced feelings of great peace and unconditional love. Some people saw religious figures, some saw dead relatives, some saw people they did not know but who definitely seemed to know them. Some people had a rapid life review. After a while, they were informed that this was not their time and they had to go back. They didn't want to go back, but the process happened anyway and they found themselves again in their body. Most of the people who underwent these near-death experiences had no subsequent fear of death and had a greater appreciation of life. They tended to become more spiritual, but not necessarily more religious.

From a reality viewpoint, the key question is: Does our consciousness survive the death of our brain? People who have had near-death experiences adamantly believe this to be true. But many scientific and medical people who have never experienced an NDE themselves say these experiences are merely delusions of a dying brain and that anyway these people did not die in actual fact. Who is right?

One scientifically-based way to begin assessing the truth here is to examine the veridicality of near-death experiences. Now the word veridical is not a commonly used one (it means "not illusory" or "genuine"). However, this word is employed in the near-death literature to denote near-death experiences that contain elements of proof that the consciousness has left the body at the time of near-death. Such veridical evidence is usually in the form of observations reported by the near-death experiencer's consciousness of events that he or she observed happening around them while in the near-death state under conditions where their physical senses could not possibly have detected what they report.

The most famous and medically well-documented veridical near-death experience is that of Pam Reynolds Lowery (31). Pam had a giant basilar artery aneurysm, a ballooned section of a large artery at the base of her brain. If the aneurysm ruptured, the result would be immediate death. So she needed a major operation to fix the problem.

The operation she had in 1991 during which her near-death experience occurred was a very radical one indeed. The surgical team would lower her body temperature to 60° Fahrenheit to induce cardiac arrest, and then drain the blood from her head so that the aneurysm could be safely removed. At the start of the aneurysm removal procedure, she would be quite clinically dead, with no heart beat and no brain waves or brainstem function.

Because this was such a major and radical type of procedure, Pam was extensively monitored during the surgery. Her eyes were taped shut. She had a catheter placed to measure pulmonary pressure and blood flow from the heart. Cardiac monitoring leads were attached to follow heart rate and rhythm, and an oximeter was taped to her index finger to measure oxygen levels in her blood. Urinary temperature was measured by a thermister placed in her bladder and the core body temperature of her inner body was measured with a thermister placed deeply into her esophagus. Her brain temperature was monitored by a thin wire embedded in its surface. She had EEG electrodes taped to her head to record cerebral cortical brain activity, and her auditory nerve center located in the brain stem was tested continuously using 100-decibel clicks at 22 clicks per second (a deep hum as loud as a jackhammer) emitted from small speakers inserted into her ears. In summary, she was fully loaded with instrumentation and diagnostics for the surgery.

Pam was placed under general anesthesia by the anesthesiologist. After ninety minutes of deep anesthesia the surgery began with the surgeon, a Dr. Spetzler, cutting out a large section of Pam's skull with a Midas Rex 73,000 rpm bone saw, which made a loud buzzing noise. Here is Pam's account of what she saw and heard when the operation began (31):

> The next thing I recall was the sound: It was a natural D. As I listened to the sound, I felt it was pulling me out of the top of my head. The further out of my body I got, the more clear the tone became. I had the impression it was like a road, a frequency that you go on . . . . I remember seeing several things in the operating room when I was looking down. It was the most aware that I think that I have ever been in my entire life . . . . I was metaphorically sitting on Dr. Spetzler's shoulder. It was not like normal vision. It was brighter and more focused and clearer than normal vision . . . . There was so much in the operating room that I didn't recognize, and so many people.
>
> I thought the way they had my head shaved was very peculiar. I expected them to take all of the hair, but they did not . . . .
>
> The saw thing that I hated the sound of looked like an electric toothbrush and it had a dent in it, a groove at the top where the saw appeared to go into the handle, but it didn't . . . . And the saw had interchangeable blades, too, but these

> blades were in what looked like a socket wrench
> case . . . . I heard the saw crank up. I didn't see
> them use it on my head, but I think I heard it
> being used on something. It was humming at a
> relatively high pitch and then all of a sudden it
> went Brrrrrrr! like that.

> Someone said something about my veins and
> arteries being very small. I believe it was a
> female voice and that it was Dr. Murray, but I'm
> not sure. She was the cardiologist. I remember
> thinking that I should have told her about
> that . . . . I remember the heart-lung machine. I
> didn't like the respirator . . . . I remember a lot
> of tools and instruments that I did not readily
> recognize.

After the operation, her surgeon Dr. Spetzler was quite astounded that she was able to describe the things she did, given the fact that she was ninety minutes into deep general anesthesia with her eyes taped shut and loud sounds in her ears. The bone saw that he had used did indeed resemble an electric toothbrush to an uninitiated person. And it did have a set of blades in a case resembling a socket wrench case. The fact is that Pam had never seen such a medical bone saw anytime in her life. And Pam was also able to hear one of the doctors talking about her veins and arteries being small, a conversation that indeed actually took place during the operation. Yet she had plugs in her ears that were giving out 100-decibel clicks like the sound of a jack hammer. She shouldn't have been able to hear a thing. So Pam Reynolds Lowery's NDE was dramatically veridical. She was providing proof that her consciousness was outside her body and aware, while her body and brain were deeply anesthetized. What does this mean for the true nature of our reality?

In the prestigious medical journal The Lancet, the following account of a near-death, out-of-body experience is given (32). This account was reported by the coronary care unit nurse:

> *During a night shift an ambulance brings a 44 year old cyanotic, comatose man into the coronary care unit. He had been found about an hour before in a meadow by passers-by. After admission, he receives artificial respiration without intubation, while heart massage and defibrillation are also applied. When we want to intubate the patient, he turns out to have dentures in his mouth. I remove these upper dentures and put them onto the 'crash cart'. Meanwhile, we continue extensive CPR. After about an hour and a half the patient has sufficient heart rhythm and blood pressure, but he is still ventilated and intubated, and he is still comatose. He is transferred to the intensive care unit to continue the necessary artificial respiration.*

> *Only after more than a week do I meet again with the patient, who is by now back on the cardiac ward. I distribute his medication. The moment he sees me he says: 'Oh, that nurse knows where my dentures are'. I am very surprised. Then he elucidates: 'Yes, you were*

there when I was brought into hospital and you took my dentures out of my mouth and put them onto that cart, it had all these bottles on it and there was this sliding drawer underneath and there you put my teeth.' I was especially amazed because I remembered this happening while the man was in deep coma and in the process of CPR. When I asked further, it appeared the man had seen himself lying in bed, that he had perceived from above how nurses and doctors had been busy with CPR. He was also able to describe correctly and in detail the small room in which he had been resuscitated as well as the appearance of those present like myself.

At the time that he observed the situation he had been very much afraid that we would stop CPR and that he would die. And it is true that we had been very negative about the patient's prognosis due to his very poor medical condition when admitted. The patient tells me that he desperately and unsuccessfully tried to make it clear to us that he was still alive and that we should continue CPR. He is deeply impressed by his experience and says he is no longer afraid of death. Four weeks later he left the hospital as a healthy man.

The nurse's account has been verified via a first-hand interview during which the nurse, identified as T.G., provided the following additional information about the patient (33):

The patient, B., from Ooy near the city of Nijmegen, had indeed been brought in on a cold night, more dead than alive . . . . He was clinically dead, period: no heartbeat, no breathing, no blood pressure, and "cold as ice" . . . . immediately after B. entered the hospital, T.G. removed the dentures from B.'s mouth and intubated him before starting up the entire reanimation procedure. Therefore, as T.G. categorically stated, any "normal" observation by the patient of his dentures being removed from his mouth was simply unthinkable.

In addition, the normal observation process could not have been the basis of the patient's detailed description of the crash cart as well as of the entire resuscitation room. Once again, T.G. was adamant in that regard, noting that patient B. had never before been in that hospital, let alone in this resuscitation room, and that this particular crash cart was absolutely unique, being a hand-made product of ramshackle quality that had been stationed in that resuscitation room only and nowhere else. To guess the precise nature of that cart and its contents on the basis of auditory impressions, or through briefly opened eyes characterized by fixed, dilated, unresponsive pupils, was impossible by all accounts. T.G. asserted that certainly it would have been impossible for B. to know precisely where T.G. had placed the dentures.

The nurse T.G. said that the patient B. was a very down-to-earth person, a steel-bender by profession. After B. was discharged from the hospital, T.G. saw him only once again when he came into the hospital for a check-up. T.G. said that B. looked like a "cardiac cripple" after his massive heart attack that almost took his life and resulted in his NDE. The nurse reported that a few years later, there was an obituary in the newspaper indicating that a B. from Ooy had died.

How can we explain this NDE account? How did the man come by the veridical information that he related to the nurse? One must remember that this is a well-documented, factual case that has been reported in a respected medical journal.

The case of Al Sullivan is also interesting from a veridical viewpoint. Sullivan was 56 years old at the time of his NDE which occurred in 1988 during a coronary bypass operation. Here is his account (34):

> *I began my journey in an upward direction and found myself in a very thick, black, billowy smoke-like atmosphere. The smoke seemed to surround me no matter what way I turned, yet it was not going to deter me as far as I was concerned . . . . As I continued on my journey, I rose to an amphitheater-like place. It had a wall directly in front of me to prevent me from going into it. Behind this wall, a very bright light shone. As I tried to get closer to this wall, I noticed three humanlike figures at my immediate left . . . . I was able to grasp*

the wall and look over it into the area the wall was blocking. To my amazement, at the lower left-hand side was, of all things, me.

I was laying [sic] on a table covered with light blue sheets and I was cut open so as to expose my chest cavity. It was in this cavity that I was able to see my heart on what appeared to be a small glass table. I was able to see my surgeon, who just moments ago had explained to me what he was going to do during my operation. He appeared to be somewhat perplexed. I thought he was flapping his arms as if trying to fly . . . .

Once Sullivan regained consciousness after the operation, he related his NDE experience to his cardiologist, a Dr. LaSala, who was present in the operating room along with the cardiac surgeon, a Dr. Takata, who had performed the actual bypass surgery. Dr. LaSala was very surprised when Sullivan described Dr. Takata as "flapping his arms as if trying to fly". LaSala explained to Sullivan that this was something Takata did in the operating room when he had not yet scrubbed in his hands, so to avoid touching the sterile operating area he would flatten his palms against his chest and use his elbows to point out instructions to assisting medical personnel. La Sala said that this did indeed look like a "flapping" motion, and that he did not know any other surgeons who employed this unusual technique.

The preceding accounts are three important cases where people in near-death medical situations have been able to see and hear things that they simply could not have with their physical senses. How did they acquire the information they reported? The only logical explanation is that their consciousness was outside their body, and had the ability to detect and remember things that were happening in the medical settings around them.

This has very profound implications indeed. These veridical NDE experiences would seem to validate the reality that "you", your consciousness, are not really just the sum total of your body and brain. And there are then the reality questions of what your consciousness truly is and where your consciousness is located when it is not in your body.

We next explore the possible reality of the out-of-body experience (OBE). Some people have reported that their consciousness can separate from their body even without the occurrence of a near-death situation. I will now cite instances where there is some degree of proof that the out-of-body experience is actually real.

Consider the case of "Miss Z". In 1968, Charles Tart, then in the Psychology Department at the University of California-Davis, reported on her case (35,36). Miss Z was a single woman in her twenties with two years of college education. Tart indicated that she had a warm personality and was highly intelligent.

Miss Z had been having OBE experiences since she was a child. In fact, as a child she thought that they were not unusual and that everyone had them. These OBEs were almost always the same for her. She would wake up during the night and find "herself" floating up at the ceiling, where she could look down and see her physical body asleep in bed. The OBE would last for less than a minute, and then she would fall back into a sleep state again.

Tart conducted sleep experiments to monitor her brain wave EEG output and other aspects such as rapid eye movements and skin resistance. He was attempting to correlate such measurements with the occurrence of OBEs. The sleep experiments took place in one room and the monitoring was done in a room immediately adjacent. Connecting the two rooms was an observation window so that the sleeping patient could be observed. Miss Z slept in a bed just below this observation window. The electrical leads from all of the various monitoring devices were bound into a common cable arrangement that went from her head to a cable connection box at the head of the bed. There was enough slack in this cable for her to turn in bed, but she could not sit up more than about two feet without breaking the cable connections. So her movements other than a few in the bed itself were severely restricted. She could not leave the bed nor could she stand up on the bed without these movements being immediately detected.

Above the observation window and about five and one-half feet above her head as she lay in bed was a small shelf. It was on this shelf that Tart placed a five-digit random number unseen by Miss Z. The objective of the experiment was for Miss Z to leave her body, float up to the ceiling, and from this vantage point observe and then recall this random number when she awoke. Tart would change to a different random number on each of the nights of his sleep experiments. Experiments were conducted on Miss Z for four consecutive nights. Here is what happened on Night 4 (35):

Miss Z went quickly to sleep, entering Stages 3 and 4 less than fifteen minutes after going to bed. The night was uneventful for the most part—there were several Stage 1 dream periods in the first two-thirds of the night, as would be expected for any normal subject. After four and a half hours of sleep, she had a Stage 1 dream period with REMs which lasted for half an hour. The EEG was technically rather poor on this night, being obscured with a great deal of sixty cycle artifact and requiring rather heavy high frequency filtering to make it clear, so the EEG findings should be taken with the realization that they are subject to more error than usual. Miss Z's Stage 1 dream terminated with several minutes of intermittent body movements and EEG artifact.

Then (at 5:50 A.M.) the occipital channel showed an enlarged, slow wave artifact, the REM channel showed no REMs, and the record looked like a Stage I tracing; however, I could not be sure due to the considerations mentioned above. At 5:57 A.M. the slow wave artifact was lessened and the record looked somewhat like Stage 1 with REMs, but I could not be sure whether this was a waking or a Stage I record. This lasted until 6:04 A.M., at which time Miss Z awoke and called out that the target number was 25132. This was correct (with the digits in correct order), but I did not say anything to her at this point; I merely indicated that I had written the number down on the record. I then told her she could go back to sleep, but twenty minutes later I awakened her so that she could get ready to go to work.

Miss Z was an interesting subject for Charles Tart indeed. On her Night 4 session, she correctly identified the five-digit random number that Tart had set, against odds of 1 in 100,000. Given this result, it is unfortunate that Tart did not perform additional extensive experimentation with Miss Z, but he did not since she subsequently moved far away from where he was located.

Charles Tart also performed OBE experiments with Robert Monroe (37), who claimed to have had extensive out-of-body experiences which began spontaneously for him in 1958 and continued throughout the rest of his life. Monroe considered himself to be something of an "explorer" of the OBE non-physical reality and published three books extensively describing his OBE experiences (38,39,40).

Tart conducted nine sleep sessions with Monroe using the same experimental monitoring techniques that he employed with Miss Z, and with the same ultimate objective of correctly identifying a five-digit random number seen during an OBE. Unfortunately, although Monroe said that he had two OBE experiences during Tart's monitoring, in neither of them was he able to see or report the random five-digit number. However, in one of his OBEs, Monroe reported the presence of Tart's technician who was with her husband in the adjacent experimental monitoring room during this sleep episode. Monroe correctly identified both she and her husband. The presence of her husband was surprising to Tart (who was not there himself at the time), since Tart had established a policy of not allowing outsiders to observe his sleeping subjects. The technician said that, against Tart's policy, her husband came to keep her company during the late night hours. Tart was not aware of this fact, but Monroe observed it during his OBE. With regard to Monroe's EEG patterns, Tart described them as "very atypical", with high intensity theta waves during periods of non-REM sleep. While it was not conclusively established, Tart believed that Monroe's stated OBEs were occurring during his non-REM sleep segments.

Robert Monroe might be considered a grand master of the out-of-body experience. He was 42 years old and president of a large company when his OBEs began spontaneously in 1958. Prior to that time, he had experienced no OBE phenomena at all. He had a business background and a scientific background as well. In other words, he was a no-nonsense guy, a solid citizen. Not the type that you would expect to be the first to document in logical, observational detail his experiences with OBEs.

Monroe was very curious and sought to explore in detail his OBEs, to understand them as best he could. He adopted a gradual, experimental approach, as a scientist might (Monroe had some level of scientific background in his education), building more understanding for himself with each additional OBE that he experienced. Monroe described experiencing three different "Locales" during his OBEs.

Locale I consisted of people and places that exist in our physical world. Monroe could travel out-of-body to different physical locations and observe the activities going on at these locations. For example, he said that one day he traveled in an out-of-body state to the home of some family friends. He observed their son on his way to school, who was tossing a ball up and down in the air as he walked along. He also saw his friend attempting to maneuver a large, bulky piece of equipment into the back seat of his car. He then observed the man and his wife distributing mail that had been delivered to each other at the kitchen table. When he subsequently visited and talked to his friends about what they had been doing on that particular day, they verified in detail what he had seen while he was out-of-body in Locale I.

Locale II, however, was completely different from Locale I and seemed to be a totally non-physical environment. Monroe described it this way (38):

> *The best introduction to Locale II is to suggest a room with a sign over the door saying, "Please Check All Physical Concepts Here".*

> *. . . . . Postulate: Locale II is a non-material environment with laws of motion and matter only remotely related to the physical world. It is an immensity whose bounds are unknown (to this experimenter), and has depth and dimension incomprehensible to the finite,*

conscious mind. In this vastness lie all of the aspects we attribute to heaven and hell, which are but a part of Locale II. It is inhabited, if that is the word, by entities with various degrees of intelligence with whom communication is possible.

. . . . Time, by the standards of the physical world, is non-existent. There is a sequence of events, a past and a future, but no cyclical separation. Both continue to exist coterminously with "now".

. . . . . Laws of conservation of energy, force field theories, wave mechanics, gravity, matter structure—all remain to be proved by those more versed in such fields.

Superseding all appears to be one prime law. Locale II is a state of being where that which we label thought is the wellspring of existence. It is the vital creative force that produces energy, assembles "matter" into form, and provides channels of perception and communication. I suspect that the very self or soul in Locale II is no more than an organized vortex or warp in this fundamental. As you think, so you are.

The third locale that Monroe described was Locale III. Here's what he said about one of his "visits" to a place in Locale III (38).

Locale III, in summary, proved to be a physical-matter world almost identical to our own. The natural environment is the same. There are trees, houses, cities, people, artifacts, and all the appurtenances of a reasonably civilized society. There are homes, families, businesses, and people work for a living. There are roads on which vehicles travel. There are railroads and trains.

Now for the "almost". At first, the thought was that Locale III was no more than some part of our world unknown to me and those others concerned. It had all the appearances of being so. However, more careful study showed that it can be neither the present nor the past of our physical-matter world.

The scientific development is inconsistent. There are no electrical devices whatsoever. Electricity, electromagnetics, and anything so related are non-existent. No electric lights, telephones, radios, television, or electric power.

Habits and customs are not like ours. What little has been gleaned implies a historical background with different events, names, places, and dates. Yet, while the stage of man's evolution (the conscious mind translates the inhabitants as men) seems to be identical, technical and social evolution are not completely the same.

The suggestion here is that Locale III may be a physical place on a planet that is not the Earth, and that the inhabitants are not human beings but rather extraterrestrials going about their everyday business on their home planet orbiting a far-away star.

In his last book, Monroe took an out-of-body "Ultimate Journey" to the source of Creation. He described our physical reality as a "holographic dream" that was generated by something he called the "Emitter" which lay behind what he termed an "Aperture". He said that our universe did not begin from a Big Bang, but rather from the emanations of the "Emitter". Furthermore, there was a closed loop from all the things in the physical universe back to the "Emitter". Everything eventually recycled to the "Emitter" and became again one with the "Whole".

Monroe described the "Creator" as being beyond the "Aperture" and the "Emitter", and that he had not journeyed to the actual site of the "Creator" during his "Ultimate Journey". So he had not seen the "Creator". However, he said in his book that the following characteristics of the "Creator" were now "knowns" to him as a result of his journey (40):

> This, our Creator: Is beyond our comprehension as long as we remain human. Is the designer of the ongoing process of which we are a part. Has a purpose for such action beyond our ability to understand. Makes adjustments, fine tuning, in this process as needed. Establishes simple laws that apply to everyone and everything. Does not demand worship, adoration, or recognition. Does not punish for "evil" and "misdeeds". Does not intercede or interdict in our life activity.

Is what Robert Monroe reported from his many OBEs credible? It is difficult to believe that Monroe's OBE accounts were pure fiction concocted for the purpose of writing and selling books about them. This would be totally inconsistent with his background, social, and financial status. What could he possibly have to gain by the publication of his OBE experiences, other than the satisfaction of communicating to other people something he sincerely believed and considered quite important. In fact, Monroe was so committed to his OBE experiences that he founded the Monroe Institute in Virginia which is dedicated to instructing people on techniques to achieve OBE states. The Monroe Institute exists to the present day, but Robert Monroe died in 1995.

Personally, I find Monroe's OBE accounts fascinating. Since Monroe did not provide any veridical evidence to substantiate his claims particularly as regarding Locales II and III, the only way to know for sure is to attempt to reproduce them on a personal experiential level. Although I have spent some time trying to do this using his meditative techniques available from the Monroe Institute, I have been unable to achieve an OBE state thus far. But who knows. I continue trying in my own meditative explorations.

We will now move to a discussion of the paranormal phenomena that classify themselves as "ghostly". There are a great many people who say that they have seen and even interacted with ghosts. The fact that so many people have reported ghostly encounters makes these phenomena difficult to dismiss simply because they do not fit into our current scientific paradigms.

What is a ghost? Many people would say that a ghost is the spirit of a person who has died but who, for some reason, is still bound to the physical plane rather than passing into the spiritual realm. A ghost does not often appear to have a physically solid body, although there are some cases where ghosts are described as looking just like normal, living people. A ghost may manifest as a solid normal person, or the transparent image of a person, or a cloud of smoky material, or as a shining orb in the air. Sometimes ghosts are reported to be able to move physical objects or to touch people physically. A few people have even reported having a conversation with a ghost.

One of the people who did just that was Elisabeth Kubler-Ross. She is now deceased herself, but is known worldwide for her books about death and dying. Kubler-Ross was a psychiatrist who did much work with dying patients. In her book "On Life after Death", she related the story of her encounter with the ghost of a Mrs. Schwarz, who was a previous patient of hers (41). Here is her account of this ghostly encounter, which happened in her office building.

Kubler-Ross was standing by the building elevator having a conversation with a colleague, when she noticed a woman who was also standing nearby. To her astonishment, this woman looked familiar to her; she looked like a Mrs. Schwarz, a patient of hers who had died ten months earlier. When her colleague left on the elevator, the woman walked over to her and said *"Dr. Ross, I had to come back. Do you mind if I walk you to your office"*. Naturally, Kubler-Ross was wondering whether or not she was hallucinating. But she walked with the woman to her office and actually touched the woman's skin during the walk to try and determine if she was real or not.

When they got to the office, the woman, not Kubler-Ross, opened the office door. This person was obviously a very solid ghost. They sat down at her desk and the woman said *"Dr. Ross, I had to come back for two reasons. One, to thank you and Reverend Gaines, to thank you and him for what you did for me. But the other reason I had to come back is that you cannot stop this work on death and dying, not yet"*. At the time of this ghostly visitation, Kubler-Ross had been seriously considering giving up her work in this area.

Wanting to get some tangible evidence of this ghostly encounter, Kubler-Ross asked the woman if she would write a note to the Reverend Gaines, and gave the ghostly woman pencil and paper. The ghost did indeed write the note. Then she got up to leave, again requesting Kubler-Ross not to give up her endeavors. When Kubler-Ross promised to her that she would not, the woman vanished into thin air!

This is a truly remarkable account of an interaction with a ghost. Not only was the ghost holding a conversation with Kubler-Ross, the ghost was also able to open a door and write a note. And this encounter comes from an international authority on death and dying. Kubler-Ross said that she still had the note that the ghostly Mrs. Schwarz had written, a solid piece of tangible evidence of her ghostly encounter.

Surveys of the general population have shown that about 15% of people have had at least once in their lifetime a sensory perception, often visual, of another person who was physically deceased. Six such encounters have been researched in detail by Stevenson (42). I will describe two of them.

E.W., a woman in Scotland, had the following apparitional experience on May 29, 1975. At about 10 am, E.W. went outside the front door of her house to pick up some delivered milk bottles and she noticed her neighbor, a Ronald McKay, walking out his driveway across the road and then down the road toward the factory where he was the manager. E.W. and her husband had known that the McKay's were away on vacation and thought they were still away. She went back into her house and casually told her husband: *"I see the McKay's are back"*. Her husband asked her when they had come back and she replied: *"I don't know, but I saw Ron go down the drive"*.

About an hour later, a senior employee of Ronald McKay's factory came to their house and informed E.W. and her husband that McKay had died at 7 am that morning while on vacation 150 miles away. Naturally, E.W. was quite taken aback by this news, but she swore she had seen a lifelike McKay walking to work that morning. She said he appeared completely solid and normal, and that she had him in view for about 10 seconds from about 50 feet away. McKay's widow reported he had died in bed in his sleep and he was naked at the time of his death since he always slept naked. Yet E.W. saw him wearing a nylon shirt tucked into flannel trousers, which McKay's wife said was his normal work attire.

The second case reported by Stevenson happened on January 4, 1965 to a girl D.I., who was 14 years old at the time. Her maternal grandfather, who was dying of leukemia, was living at her home along with the other members of her family. The apparition occurred while she was alone in the house with her grandfather. This is her account of it (42):

> *Granddaddy called to me to give him a drink of water. I failed in my attempts to lift him enough to wet his lips. The disease had reduced his once tall, strong stature to a frail, weak invalid. I called mom at work to ask for help, but she told me it would have to wait until dad returned from work at noon. Shortly thereafter I heard granddaddy calling out to his wife, Hazel. Grandmom had died nine years prior (on October 13, 1956), so I thought he must be losing his mind. I ran down the hall to make another attempt to help him. I was amazed to find him sitting up, smiling with his arms reaching out. The room was filled with a warm, bright light. He spoke to grandmom, who was standing at the foot of his bed. Neither of them acknowledged my presence. She was there but a brief moment, and when granddaddy laid back down, his soul escaped with her. He died with a smile on his face.*
>
> *And I can still visualize it. If this was the room and his bed was here the light came out of that corner there of the ceiling and it came, shone right down at the very foot of his bed. And she was not on the floor. She, her, I didn't see her feet. But she was above the floor. And if*

a conversation was held between them it was not to my ears. You could see very beautiful, peaceful expressions on their faces. That is the most vivid part of it for me. That they both were just so at peace at seeing each other. And he raised up. By the time I get to the room he didn't even acknowledge that I had come to the room. He raises up and he raised his arms up to reach her and he just laid back. And when he laid back down he had a smile on his face and his eyes were open. And she. When I am looking at him, then I look back and she was gone. And I got hysterical because I knew without even knowing how. I didn't know how to check for vital signs or anything. I just knew that he was dead. That he had passed.

In addition to these ghostly apparitions, there are also poltergeist phenomena that many ordinary people report happening to them. Poltergeist is a German word meaning "noisy ghost". Most reports of poltergeist manifestations involve noises or movements that have no immediate or verifiable cause. Situations include inanimate objects being picked up or moved, noises such as knocking, rapping, or human voices, and even physical attacks on human beings in some relatively rare cases.

In the 19th century, the most important and best documented case of poltergeist phenomena is associated with the famous medium Daniel Dunglas Home. Descriptions provided by witnesses of the phenomena that occurred in his presence are impressive indeed. In Home's presence, large and heavy objects such as tables were suspended in mid-air with no possible means of support. Superb musical arrangements were played on an accordion Home held in only one of his hands, with the other end of the accordion seemingly moving by itself. Apparitions of apparently solid hands and arms appeared that would touch people in his vicinity (however, there was never a full-body solid apparition that occurred in Home's presence). Finally and most spectacularly, many witnesses reported Home was able to levitate himself and move around freely in the air with no visible means of support.

Of significant importance is the fact that the psychic phenomena displayed by Daniel Dunglas Home were studied scientifically by Sir William Crookes. William Crookes was one of the most distinguished scientists of the nineteenth and early twentieth centuries. He was both a physicist and a chemist, and the discoverer of the chemical element thallium. Crookes also invented the radiometer and the cathode ray tube. He served as President of the British Royal Society, the Chemical Society, the Institution of Electrical Engineers, and the Society of Chemical Industry. Crookes was elected a Fellow of the Royal Society in 1863, received the Royal Gold Medal in 1875, the Davy Medal in 1888, the Sir Joseph Copley Medal in 1904, and the Order of Merit in 1910. He was knighted for his scientific achievements in 1897. To sum up, William Crookes was indisputably a world-class scientist of his day.

Crookes became interested in spiritualist phenomena in 1869. His original motivation was to debunk such phenomena by making rigorous scientific observations of them. It was in this context that he became involved with the spiritualist D.D. Home, and began to conduct experiments on the spiritualist phenomena Home displayed. Crookes published a summary of his experimental observations with Home in the January 1874 issue of the Quarterly Journal of Science (43). Here are some of his first-hand scientific observations of phenomena that occurred under carefully controlled conditions in Crookes' own house:

> The instances in which heavy bodies, such as tables, chairs, sofas, etc., have been moved, when the medium has not been touching them, are very numerous. I will briefly mention a few of the most striking. My own chair has been twisted partly round, whilst my feet were off the floor. A chair was seen by all present to move slowly up to the table from a far corner, when all were watching it; on another occasion an arm chair moved to where we were sitting, and then moved slowly back again (a distance of about three feet) at my request.

> On five separate occasions a heavy dining-table rose between a few inches and 1 1/2 feet off the floor, under special circumstances which rendered trickery impossible. On another occasion a heavy table rose from the floor in full light, while I was holding the medium's hands and feet. On another occasion the table rose from the floor, not only when no person was touching it, but under conditions which I had prearranged so as to assure unquestionable proof of the fact.

The most striking cases of levitation which I have witnessed have been with Mr. Home. On three separate occasions have I seen him raised completely from the floor of the room. Once sitting in an easy chair, once kneeling on his chair, and once standing up. On each occasion I had full opportunity of watching the occurrence as it was taking place . . . . The accumulated testimony establishing Mr. Home's levitations is overwhelming.

A medium, walking into my dining room, cannot, while seated in one part of the room with a number of persons keenly watching him, by trickery make an accordion play in my own hand when I hold it keys downwards, or cause the same accordion to float about the room playing all the time.

Under the strictest test conditions, I have seen a solid self-luminous body, the size and nearly the shape of a turkey's egg, float noiselessly about the room, at one time higher than any one present could reach standing on tiptoe, and then gently descend to the floor. It was visible for more than ten minutes, and before it faded away it struck the table three times with a sound like that of a hard solid body. During this time the medium was lying back, apparently insensible, in an easy chair.

A beautifully formed small hand rose up from an opening in a dining-table and gave me a flower; it appeared and then disappeared three times at intervals, affording me ample opportunity of satisfying myself that it was as real in appearance as my own. This occurred in the light in my own room, whilst I was holding the medium's hands and feet.

A hand has been repeatedly seen by myself and others playing the keys of an accordion, both of the medium's hands being visible at the same time, and sometimes being held by those near him. The hands and fingers do not always appear to me to be solid and life-like . . . . I have more than once seen, first an object move, then a luminous cloud appear to form about it, and, lastly, the cloud condense into a shape and become a perfectly-formed hand. At this stage the hand is visible to all present. It is not always a mere form, but sometimes appears perfectly life-like and graceful, the fingers moving, and the flesh apparently as human as that of any in the room. At the wrist, or arm, it becomes hazy, and fades off into a luminous cloud. To the touch, the hand sometimes appears icy cold and dead, at other times, warm and life-like, grasping my own with the firm pressure of an old friend. I have retained one of these hands in my own, firmly resolved not to let it escape. There was no struggle or effort made to get loose, but it gradually seemed to resolve itself into vapour, and faded in that manner from my grasp.

A luminous hand came down from the upper part of the room, and after hovering near me for a few seconds, took the pencil from my hand, rapidly wrote on a sheet of paper, threw the pencil down, and then rose up over our heads, gradually fading into darkness.

The following is a still more striking instance. As in the former case, Mr. Home was the medium. A phantom form came from a corner of the room, took an accordion in its hand, and then glided about the room playing the instrument. The form was visible to all present for many minutes, Mr. Home also being seen at the same time. Coming rather close to a lady who was sitting apart from the rest of the company, she gave a slight cry, upon which it vanished.

I speak chiefly of Mr. Home, as he is so much more powerful than most of the mediums I have experimented with. But with all I have taken such precautions as to place trickery out of the list of possible explanations.

It is obvious that a "medium" possesses a something which is not possessed by an ordinary being. Give this something a name. Call it 'x' if you like. Mr. Serjeant Cox calls it Psychic Force.

This is the force to which the name of Psychic Force has been given by me as properly

> *designating a force which I thus contend to be*
> *traced back to the Soul or Mind of the Man as*
> *its source. The difference between the advocates*
> *of Psychic Force and the Spiritualists consists*
> *in this—that we contend that there is as yet*
> *insufficient proof of any other directing agent*
> *than the Intelligence of the Medium, and no*
> *proof whatever of the agency of Spirits of the*
> *Dead; while the Spiritualists hold it as a faith,*
> *not demanding further proof, that Spirits of the*
> *Dead are the sole agents in the production of*
> *all the phenomena.*

Crookes ascribed these phenomena to the action of a scientifically unknown "Psychic Force". The scientific community rejected the validity of these experiments, but Crookes, the world-class scientist, had absolute confidence in the reality of his scientific observations of these effects until the day he died.

Perhaps the most famous and well-documented recent poltergeist case is that of the Rosenheim Poltergeist, which took place in Rosenheim, Bavaria. Equipment in the office of a lawyer was observed to operate by itself from summer 1967 to January 1968.

The lights in the office were reported to have turned off and on by themselves, telephones to have rung without anyone apparently calling, photocopiers to have spilled their copier fluid, and desk drawers to have opened without being touched. Post clerks installed instruments that recorded numerous phone calls which never made. Within five weeks the instruments recorded roughly

600 calls despite the fact that all the phones in the office were disabled. In October 1967 all the office light bulbs went out simultaneously with a loud bang. Pictures on the wall were actually filmed rotating around their hooks. And finally, a heavy filing cabinet is reported to have been pushed across the floor by some invisible force.

The police and the electric company were both called in to try and determine the source of the poltergeist phenomena, but were unsuccessful. Then, a team of well-known scientists was asked to research the phenomena in search of an explanation. They installed cameras and recording devices and were able to determine that the poltergeist events only happened when a nineteen-year-old recently hired secretary by the name of Annemarie Schneider was present. It was thus concluded that Miss Schneider was somehow catalyzing the phenomena, but they were unable to discover how. In the end, the poltergeist phenomena ceased completely when Ms. Schneider was dismissed from the law office.

The next topic in our discussion of unexplained reality is extrasensory perception (ESP). The term extrasensory perception encompasses phenomena such as clairvoyance (being able to "see" things that it is not possible for the eyes to physically see), psychokinesis (being able to move or affect objects using only the mind), telepathy (mind-to-mind communication), and precognition (the ability to predict future events).

In his book "The Conscious Universe", Dean Radin summarized many of the scientific studies that have been performed to determine if ESP phenomena are real effects or not (44). The type of analysis employed is called meta-analysis, where the units of the overall statistical evaluation are independent ESP investigations that have been performed by various different investigators. Hundreds of studies conducted with considerable scientific rigor in the 20th century were evaluated. Radin's meta-analysis results convincingly show that clairvoyance, telepathy, and psychokinesis are real effects that produce statistically significant results above those predicted by chance. All of the studies in the meta-analyses were of the double-blind type (i.e. the correct answer was not known by either the investigators or the subjects involved in the experiments).

Investigations of telepathy typically involve a "sender" attempting to send a mental image of a viewed image to a "receiver". In many investigations, when telepathic receivers were isolated by heavy-duty electromagnetic and magnetic shielding (specially constructed rooms with steel and copper walls) or by extreme distance, they were still able to obtain information from the sender. The most interesting telepathy studies are those that employ the so-called "ganzfeld" technique. Here, a person is placed into a condition of sensory isolation; they are lying down in a silent, soundproof room and their eyes are covered. The purpose of the sensory isolation is to increase the likelihood of detecting faint mental perceptions that might otherwise be obscured by normal sensory inputs.

In the case of clairvoyance, the situation is similar except there is no person who is a "sender"; rather the "receiver" attempts to mentally "view" an image that has been concealed from his sight. The image may be in the same room as the "receiver", say inside a sealed opaque envelope, or it may be in a sealed envelope that is physically located at a different location completely.

Psychokinesis studies typically involve attempting to use a person's will to influence the roll of a dice or the result of a binary random number generator that randomly generates either "1"s or "0"s. The random number generator experiments are particularly compelling since they do not involve a physical object such as a dice but rather just a computer generated number.

Meta-analysis studies have shown that in the case of clairvoyance and telepathy, correct "hits" are obtained approximately 60% of the time (as compared to a 50% chance hit rate) and for psychokinesis 51% of the time (as compared to a 50% chance hit rate).While these percentages may seem relatively small to you, because of the large size of the statistical samples, the odds of their happening by chance alone are extremely low, of the order of 1,000,000,000,000-to-1. Such results clearly demonstrate that these ESP phenomena are real phenomena and not something metaphysical. It should be noted that even the highly skeptical scientist Carl Sagan thought the ganzfeld telepathy results and the random number generator psychokinesis results deserved to be seriously considered.

While quite definitive in terms of scientifically establishing the reality of ESP phenomena, these statistical analyses are somewhat dry in character and do not provide much insight into the characteristics of the phenomena that are being exhibited. One can get a much better feel for these phenomena through more detailed descriptions of some of the more startling ESP cases. We will now do this for the cases of clairvoyance and psychokinesis.

Clairvoyance is a French word which translates as "clear vision". Perhaps the most interesting clairvoyance phenomena are associated with the remote viewing programs that were conducted in both the United States and the former Soviet Union.

In the early 1970's, clairvoyance experiments being conducted in the USSR prompted the U.S. government to establish experiments on remote viewing that might be used for obtaining sensitive and important information on potential enemy activities. In the fall of 1972, a remote viewing program was begun under the aegis of the CIA at Stanford Research Institute in California by two laser physicists, Dr. Hal Puthoff and Dr. Russell Targ. The first remote viewer in this program was a New York artist and psychic by the name of Ingo Swann. Ingo Swann displayed a very high level of remote viewing capabilities, and was a key member of the initial remote viewing team. The code name for these CIA remote viewing activities was Stargate.

Ingo Swann might be described as a rather colorful person (he published elements of his autobiography on the internet in 1996 (45)). This starts with his name, Ingo Swann, which is his real name. You just don't find that many people who have a first name of Ingo, and his full name Ingo Swann definitely suggests something exotic. Then there is the location of his birth, Telluride, Colorado where he was born in 1933. Now, I don't know how many of you have been to Telluride, but it is one of the most scenic mountain locations in all of Colorado (along with its sister town Ouray, which is right across the mountain from Telluride). Telluride is a mountain resort area now but in 1933, at the height of the Great Depression, it was a very small mining town with a population of only 150.

Ingo had a relatively normal and apparently happy childhood. He was something of an introvert and also a voracious book reader. And he was very intelligent and curious about the nature of things. He graduated from college with a B.A. degree in 1955 and after that enlisted in the Army rather than being drafted. He spent most of his three-year Army tour in Korea and the Far East and upon leaving the Army settled in New York City with the goal of becoming an artist and painter. However, he quickly discovered that there were many "starving artists" in Gotham and so, to put bread on the table, he worked at the United Nations for twelve years. After that, he went back to painting and was able to at least subsist on the sale of his works.

While in New York, he made social contacts with people who were interested in paranormal phenomena and this eventually led him to become a test subject for the American Society for Psychical Research (ASPR). His initial experimentation was targeted at attempting to alter the temperature reading of an isolated and sealed thermistor, a device for precisely measuring temperature, by using only his mind. In these experiments, he achieved some success, enough for a publication in the Journal of the American Society for Psychical Research. This also brought him to the attention of the CIA. As Ingo said in his memoir (45): "*A confirmed example of controlled psychokinetic effects had been demonstrated by a subject in a laboratory. If he can trigger a thermistor could he not also trigger a nuclear bomb?*"

At the ASPR, Ingo began experiments in 1971 with what was termed "remote viewing". It should be noted that in these experiments, Swann was more than just a guinea pig with psychic abilities. He actively participated in the design, conduct, and interpretation of the results and was instrumental in the development of a methodology for remote viewing.

The initial remote viewing methodology was quite simple. A number of sealed envelopes were created, each one containing the name of a U.S. city as well as the phone number of the weather service in that city. One of the sealed envelopes was selected by an ASPR person, who did not know its contents in advance. Then the name of the city was communicated to Ingo who was sitting in a chair with his head wired up to an EEG machine. Here is how Ingo Swann described the first successful remote viewing experiment (45):

> *Thus, after the morning and afternoon OOB practice sessions on December 8, 1971, and while I was still hooked up to the brainwave contraption, another ASPR worker, Vera Feldman, then handed Janet Mitchell a sealed envelope.*
>
> *Through the intercom Janet said (I remember her words very clearly): "Ingo, I've got the envelope. Let me know when you're ready."*

"I'm ready," I replied, even though I was also quite nervous.

So through the intercom I could her Janet tearing open the envelope. Then she breathed hard and said: "The target is Tucson, Arizona."

Now something wondrous and magical occurred.

Of course I really had no idea how to "get" to Tucson from the rather ugly experimental room in New York. And when I first heard the mention of "Tucson, Arizona," a picture of hot desert flashed through my mind.

But then I had the sense of moving, a sense that lasted but a fraction of a second. Some part of my head or brain or perceptions blacked out—and THERE I was—THERE. Zip, Bang, Pop—and there I was . . . something I would refer to years ahead as "immediate transfer of perceptions."

So fast was the whole of this, or so it seemed to me, that I began speaking almost as soon as Janet had narrated the distant site through the intercom.

"Am over a wet highway, buildings nearby and in the distance. The wind is blowing. It's cold. And it is raining hard."

I didn't even have time to sketch this, for it was easy enough to articulate into the tape recorder.

Having said as much, I noted that there was water glistening on the highway—and then said: "That's it! Tucson's having a fucking big rainstorm," although the forbidden word was not entered into the record of the experiment.

"That's it?" questioned Janet through the intercom. "Yeah, that's it—only that I'm slightly dizzy. I thought this would take longer. It's raining and very cold there."

"Okay," Janet replied, again breathing hard. Through the intercom I heard her dialing the number of the weather service in Tucson.

I was sweating, and started to pull off the electrodes. I noticed that my spine was tingling—if that's the correct word.

Before I could stand up, though, Janet said through the intercom: "Well, you're right on, baby. Right now Tucson is having unexpected thunderstorms and the temperature is near freezing."

I remember all of this with extreme clarity, largely because it was my first consciously experienced Zap-Pop biolocation thing. It is indelibly etched somewhere in "my mind."
It wasn't until I got home that evening that I realized while "at" Tucson I had completely lost perceptual and sensory contact with the

*experimental room at the ASPR—even with
my own body.*

*And I had no idea at all that this simple small
thing would eventually lead into a very big thing,
indeed—and into circumstances which were so
unusual that they bewildered very many.*

That is how Ingo Swann described the beginning of the
phenomenon of remote viewing. Now the story moves to
the Stanford Research Institute in California.

Following Ingo's first remote viewing experience at ASPR,
he began to have difficulties with that organization.
Perhaps the foremost difficulty was that the organization's
journal declined to publish any of the remote viewing
results that had been generated. There was also some
friction due to the fact that Swann had associations with
the Scientology movement.

In March 1972, Swann had occasion to read a document
that was written by Dr. Harold E. Puthoff, a laser physicist
working at the Stanford Research Institute in Menlo Park,
California. SRI was a government-supported organization
with links to the Defense Department and the CIA. This
document was a proposal to do some research in the
area of quantum biology. Swann was so impressed with
the content of Puthoff's document that he sat down
and wrote Puthoff a letter saying that he was interested
in investigating the boundary between the animate and
the inanimate. Ingo also described some of the research
results that had been obtained by him at ASPR.

When Puthoff received Swann's letter, he was intrigued by the results Swann had achieved in the ASPR work and was impressed enough to invite Swann to visit SRI for a week in June 1972 so that he could try and test Swann's psychic abilities.

Puthoff decided to put Swann's abilities to the test by having him attempt to influence the behavior of a very-well-shielded (physically, electrically, and magnetically), superconducting Josephson junction magnetometer that was being employed in a cutting-edge research experiment on quark-detection in the Physics Department at Stanford University. Swann was not informed of this test in advance, but he agreed to attempt it.

To Puthoff's amazement, Swann was actually able to perturb the output of the heavily shielded magnetometer. Furthermore, Swann went on to "remote view" the interior of the apparatus, providing a drawing that described reasonably accurately its construction. Puthoff wrote up these observations and circulated them to some of his scientific colleagues.

A couple of weeks later, Puthoff had a visit from two people with CIA credentials. They told him that there was increasing concern at the CIA about the level of effort in Soviet parapsychology that was being supported by Soviet security organizations. In other words, they were worried about Soviet psychic spying capabilities. They asked Puthoff if they could have the opportunity to carry out some simple experiments themselves under Puthoff's oversight and he agreed. These experiments involved hiding objects in a box and asking Swann to try and describe the contents of the box. Swann's results were impressive enough to the CIA people that in short order Puthoff had a $50,000 remote viewing research grant from them, for which he enlisted the involvement of a laser colleague Russell Targ who had an interest in the paranormal. That, according to Puthoff, was the beginning of the CIA remote viewing program. In 1995, the program was "officially ended" by the CIA, who claimed that it did not yield significant results. However, it is much more likely that these activities continue under the cover of "black projects" completely hidden from any public view. In 1996, Puthoff published an article on the CIA-sponsored remote viewing activities, since aspects of these activities had been declassified (46).

The scientists Puthoff and Targ were truly dumbfounded by Swann's remote viewing abilities. Swann showed them that he could observe what was going on at a remote location that was identified to him only by its geographic latitude and longitude map coordinates. When Swann proposed trying this, they did not believe it was possible, given the fact that map coordinates are just a man-made construct used for convenience in finding points on a map. But to their great surprise Ingo was able to "go" to a remote location that was given to him with only latitude and longitude map coordinates.

Here the remote viewing experiment that was most impressive to Puthoff and Targ in terms of what Swann was capable of (47):

> *"Ingo," we begin, "a skeptical colleague of ours on the East Coast has heard of your ability to*

*close your eyes and observe a scene miles away.
He has furnished us with a set of coordinates,
latitude and longitude, in degrees, minutes,
and seconds, and has challenged us to describe
what's there. We ourselves don't know what the
answer is. Do you think you can do it, right
off the top of your head?" "I'll try," says Ingo,
appearing unperturbed by a request that we, as
physicists, can hardly believe we are making.*

*For us, this is a crucial test. We are certain there
is no possibility of collusion between the subject
and the challenger. The coordinates indicate a
site that is roughly 3,000 miles away, and we
have been asked to obtain details beyond what
would ever be shown on any map, such as small
man-made structures, buildings, roads, etc.*

*Ingo closes his eyes and begins to describe what
he is visualizing, opening his eyes from time to
time to sketch a map. "This seems to be some
sort of mounds or rolling hills. There is a city
to the north; I can see taller buildings and
some smog. This seems to be a strange place,
somewhat like the lawns that one would find
around a military base, but I get the impression
that there are either some old bunkers around,
or maybe this is a covered reservoir. There
must be a flagpole, some highways to the west,
possibly a river over to the far east, to the south
more city." He appears to zero in for a closer
view, rapidly sketching a detailed map showing
the location of several buildings, together with*

*some roads and trees. He goes on: "Cliffs to
the east, fence to the north. There's a circular
building, perhaps a tower, buildings to the
south. Is this a former Nike base or something
like that?"*

A few weeks after Swann's remote viewing description,
Puthoff and Targ received a phone call from their East
Coast colleague who verified the accuracy of all the
details Swann had provided about the physical site
three thousand miles away. Needless to say, these two
hard-nosed scientists were astounded and believed that
they were dealing with a phenomenon inexplicable by the
science that they knew.

In 1973 another extraordinary remote reviewing
experiment was conducted by Swann, Puthoff, and Targ.
The objective was to attempt to have the remote viewer
(Swann) "go" to the planet Jupiter and observe what he
could at that extraterrestrial location. The reason for
this experiment was to test the extreme distance limits
of remote viewing in a way that might be scientifically
verifiable. Now in 1973 there was a Pioneer spacecraft on
its way to Jupiter, Pioneer 10. Pioneer 10 was the very first
spacecraft to have a close encounter flyby with Jupiter,
which happened in November 1973. So it would be
possible to compare the remote viewing results with the
observations taken of Jupiter by Pioneer 10. The Jupiter
remote viewing experiment was conducted on April 27,
1973, six months before Pioneer 10 was near enough to
Jupiter to transmit any data.

The experiment began at 6:00 pm and the first
impressions that Swann got of the planet occurred at

6:03 pm. This time difference was noted because it was thought it might relate to the speed of the remote viewing phenomenon. Here is the actual information that was transmitted verbally from Swann to his transcriber, Hal Puthoff (48):

6:03:25 *"There's a planet with stripes."*

6:04:13 *"I hope it's Jupiter."*

> *"I think that it must have an extremely large hydrogen mantle. If a space probe made contact with that, it would be maybe 80,000-120,000 miles out from the planet surface."*

> 6:06 *"So I'm approaching it on the tangent where I can see it's a half-moon, in other words, half-lit/half-dark. If I move around to the lit side, it's distinctly yellow toward the right."*

(Hal: *"Which direction you had to move?"*)

> 6:06:20 *"Very high in the atmosphere there are crystals . . . they glitter. Maybe the stripes are like bands of crystals, maybe like rings of Saturn, though not far out like that. Very close within the atmosphere.*

> *[Note: See sketch of ring in the raw data drawing below.] (Unintelligible sentence.) I bet you they'll reflect radio probes. Is that*

possible if you had a cloud of crystals that were assaulted by different radio waves?"

(Hal: "That's right.")

6:08:00 *"Now I'll go down through. It feels really good there (laughs). I said that before, didn't I? Inside those cloud layers, those crystal layers, they look beautiful from the outside. From the inside they look like rolling gas clouds—eerie yellow light, rainbows."*

6:10:20 *"I get the impression, though I don't see, that it's liquid."*

6:10:55 *"Then I came through the cloud cover. The surface—it looks like sand dunes. They're made of very large grade crystals, so they slide. Tremendous winds, sort of like maybe the prevailing winds of Earth, but very close to the surface of Jupiter. From that view, the horizon looks orangish or rose-colored, but overhead it's kind of greenish-yellow."*

6:12:35 *"If I look to the right there is an enormous mountain range."*

6:13:18 *"If I'm giving a description of where I've gone and am, it would be approximately where Alaska is if the sun were directly overhead, which it is. The*

sun looks like it has a green corona . . .
seems smaller to me.

(Hal: "What color is the sun?")

"White."

6:14:45 "I feel that there's liquid somewhere.
Those mountains are very huge but they
still don't poke up through the crystal
cloud cover. You know I had a dream once
something like this, where the cloud cover
was a great arc . . . sweeps over the entire
heaven. Those grains which make that
sand orange are quite large. They have a
polished surface and they look something
like amber or like obsidian but they're
yellowish and not as heavy. The wind
blows them. They slide along."

6:16:37 "If I turn, the whole thing seems
enormously flat. I mean, if I get the feeling
that if a man stood on those sands, I think
he would sink into them (laughs). Maybe
that's where that liquid feeling comes from."

6:18:10 "I see something that looks like a
tornado. Is there a thermal inversion here?
I bet there is. I bet you that the surface of
Jupiter will give a very high infrared count
(?), reading (?)

(Hal: "Reading . . . inaudible sentence.)

"The heat is held down."

6:19:55 "I seem to be stuck, not moving. I'll move more towards the equator. I get the impression that that must be a band of crystals similar to the outer ones, kind of bluish. They seem to be sort of in orbit, permanent orbit, down through another layer farther down which are like our clouds but moving fast. There's another area: liquid like water. Looks like it's got icebergs in it, but they're not icebergs."

6:22:20 "Tremendous wind. It's colder here, maybe it's because there's not a thermal inversion there."

6:23:25 "I'm back. OK." (Hal: "Very interesting.")

"The atmosphere of Jupiter is very thick. I mean . . . (Ingo draws) . . . Explanation of drawing: This is what appears to be a hydrogen mantle about 100,000 miles off the surface. Those here are bands of crystals, kind of elements. They're pretty close to the surface. And beneath those are layers of clouds or what seem to be prevailing winds. Beneath that is the surface which I saw was, well, it looked like shifting sands made out of some sort of slippery granulated stuff. And off in the distance, I guess, to the East was a very high mountain chain 30,000 feet or so,

> quite large mountains. I feel these crystals
> will probably bounce radio waves. They're
> that type.

Generally, that's all."

Swann's "trip" to Jupiter was only 23 minutes in length. However, he reported some startling things. He said that Jupiter had a ring around it, something like the rings of Saturn. This caused Hal Puthoff to wonder if Swann had gone to the wrong planet. It also caused Puthoff's astronomer colleagues to scoff, since no rings around Jupiter had ever been seen by Earth telescopes, and additionally the Pioneer 10 Jupiter flyby later that year did not show any Jupiter rings. But, and this is a very interesting "but", the later Voyager probes of Jupiter in 1979 with their much better photographic resolutions than Pioneer 10, did indeed show that there was a ring around Jupiter. So Swann's remote viewing observation was actually correct. I find this to be quite remarkable.

More startling than the ring, however, was Swann's report that Jupiter had a solid core beneath its cloud layers. He said that there appeared to be solid "mountains" and liquid-appearing regions. Now this made the astronomers in 1973 really derisive, since at that time the consensus was that Jupiter was totally gaseous, with no solid core. Yet, things have changed between 1973 and the present. Astronomers now keep open the possibility of a solid core because it might be related to the intense magnetic field that surrounds Jupiter. In fact, in August 2011 NASA launched the Juno probe to Jupiter. When it reaches Jupiter in 2016, one of its tasks is to determine whether or not Jupiter has a solid core. If it does, the solid must be solid hydrogen and/or helium, and possibly also liquid forms of these elements. Wouldn't it be interesting if Ingo Swann were proven right about this as well?

In addition to the work that Puthoff and Targ did with Ingo Swann, they also investigated the remote viewing abilities of other subjects. Their results with three other subjects, Uri Geller, Pat Price, and Hella Hammid, were published in the distinguished scientific journal Nature in 1974. The conclusions of their published Nature article were the following (49):

> *From these experiments we conclude that:*
>
> *A channel exists whereby information about a remote location can be obtained by means of an as yet unidentified perceptual modality.*
>
> *As with all biological systems, the information channel appears to be imperfect, containing noise along with signal.*
>
> *While a quantitative signal-to-noise ratio in the information-theoretical sense cannot as yet be determined, the results of our experiments indicate that the functioning is at the level of useful information transfer.*
>
> *It may be that remote perceptual ability is widely distributed in the general population, but because the perception is generally below an individual's level of awareness, it is repressed or not noticed.*

This last conclusion from Targ and Puthoff's *Nature* article is most interesting. In their studies, they were able to show that many people have an innate capability to exhibit the remote viewing phenomenon. Perhaps even you and I.

Let's now move to a discussion of psychokinesis, which is a Greek word meaning "mind movement".

As was previously described, Ingo Swann not only demonstrated clairvoyant remote viewing abilities, but also psychokinetic abilities as well. At the American Society for Psychical Research, he was able to affect the temperature of an isolated and sealed thermistor. At the Stanford Research Institute, he demonstrated the ability to influence the signal generated by an isolated and sealed magnetometer.

What other individuals have exhibited significant psychokinetic abilities? The name that immediately comes to mind is Uri Geller and his psychokinetic spoon-bending ability. Geller was born in Israel in 1946 and here is how Geller described his first spoon-bending experience in the late 1950's in his autobiography (50):

> One time my mother had made some mushroom soup. There was good white bread with the soup, and I dipped the bread into it and ate. Then I started eating the soup with my spoon. I'm left-handed, so I held the spoon in my left hand and took several sips of the soup. My mother was standing by the kitchen stove. I was lifting a full spoonful up to my mouth,

*when suddenly the bowl of the spoon bent
down and spilled hot soup into my lap. Then
the bowl of the spoon itself fell off. I was left
there holding the handle.*

Geller was in the Israeli army at the time of the 1967
Arab-Israeli war. He experienced significant personal
combat as a foot soldier and was seriously wounded,
but he fully recovered. After he was discharged from the
army, he needed to establish a means of making a living.
Since he was an outgoing person and had a talent for
performance, Geller began to give public demonstrations
of metal-bending in various locations within Israel. He
stated that having an audience seemed to help him with
his metal-bending abilities. However, at one point Geller
said his manager urged him to include magician's tricks
in addition to his metal-bending demonstrations so as to
lengthen the performance and make it more interesting
to the viewing public. This he reluctantly did, but in
retrospect he said it was a very big mistake on his part,
because many people came to believe his metal-bending
abilities were in actual fact just magician's tricks as well.

So Geller was making a living as a small-time stage
performer at various locations in Israel. But then he came
into contact with Dr. Andrija Puharich in November
1971, an event that changed his life dramatically. Puharich
was a U.S. medical doctor who also had a great interest in
paranormal phenomena. He had heard about Geller's stage
shows through the grapevine and became so interested
that he traveled from the U.S. to Tel Aviv in Israel to meet
Geller in person. He wanted to personally conduct some
scientific experiments to evaluate Geller's abilities. This

is Puharich's description of his initial interaction with Geller (51):

> We will do a telepathy test in which I will think of a three-digit number, and you will try to guess what these numerals are. You take this blank pad and pencil and go into the next room. I will stay here with a pad and pencil. When I say 'Go,' I will write down three digits, and at the same time you will write down the first three digits that come to your mind. Is this clear?"

> "Yes, I understand," said Uri, as he took the pad and pencil and went to the next room. I shouted "Go" and without thinking, wrote down "6 3 1" on my pad. Uri came out of the room a minute later and said, "That is very fast; I usually work much slower. But here is my paper."
> I laid his paper alongside my paper: Mine: 6 3 1; Uri's: 6 3 1. . . . .

> My first experiment was to see if Uri had the power to move a magnetic compass needle solely by mental effort. I had two liquid-filled compasses as the test instruments. Uri had never before tried to move a compass needle, so he was very unsure of himself. Before the tests began he gave me permission to search his body for any hidden devices; I found nothing. On the first try, after some seven minutes of concentration, Uri was able to move a compass needle sixteen degrees clockwise. We both felt

that this was not impressive, but that he did have potential in this area.

Then I tested his power to "bend" a thin stream of water falling from a water tap when his hand was brought near it. This is purely an electrostatic effect, which anyone can bring about with an electrically charged plastic comb, but very few people accomplish it solely with a finger. Uri was able to bend the water stream when he brought his dry finger near the stream of water. But he could not bend it when his finger or hand was wet with water; wetting his skin seemed to neutralize the electrical charge on his skin.

On the twenty-fourth I started an additional series of tests. I was interested to find out whether Uri could control his mind energy in a narrow beam, or whether he used his energy in a kind of shotgun "scatter beam." My experiment was a simple one. I prepared five wooden matches of equal length and weight and placed them in a long row, end to end. The matches were on a glass plate monitored by a movie camera. Uri's task was to concentrate on the five matches and then try to move any match or group of matches that I selected.

On the first try Uri was able to make the match that I selected move forward some thirty-two millimeters. On succeeding tries he was able to move any match that I selected while the

> others remained stationary. When moved by
> his Mindpower, the matches always moved by
> jumping forward like a frog jumps. I concluded
> from these tests that Uri could in fact control
> the beam spread of his mental energy.

Puharich wanted to try and understand how Geller
had acquired his abilities, so he hypnotized him. Under
hypnosis, Geller remembered that in 1949 as a child of
three he had had an interaction in a garden in Tel Aviv
with an extraterrestrial being and Geller stated that he
had been given his abilities as a result of this interaction.
Under further hypnosis, Geller spoke with a strange voice
and said the following:

> Andrija, you shall take care of Uri. Take good
> care of him. He is in a very delicate situation. He
> is the only one for the next fifty years to come.
> We are going to be very, very far away. Spectra,
> Spectra, Spectra: That is our spacecraft.

So, strange as it may seem, under hypnosis Geller seemed
to channel communications with extraterrestrial
beings who were located on a spacecraft call "Spectra".
When Puharich asked the hypnotized Geller how far
away the spacecraft was located, the strange voice
said that it was 53,069 "light-ages" (light-years?) away
from Earth.

Despite the highly unusual things spoken about
extraterrestials by Geller under hypnosis, the experiments
he conducted with Geller impressed Puharich enough
that he made arrangements for Geller to come to the U.S.

so that scientists could do more controlled experiments on him. In October 1972, Uri Geller visited the Stanford Research Institute to allow Hal Puthoff and Russell Targ to scientifically investigate his alleged spoon-bending abilities. Their objective was to have Geller demonstrate that he could bend spoons without touching them himself. In other words, what they wanted to do was to have the spoon be physically located in a sealed and evacuated bell jar, and then observe its bending under the remote action of Geller's mind (47).

Once Geller arrived at SRI, he certainly exhibited a whole collection of strange phenomena that impressed Puthoff and Targ, but unfortunately were not conducted under rigorous scientific controls. For example, immediately upon his arrival he insisted on driving Puthoff and Targ around the local Palo Alto area while he was blindfolded. And in fact he did manage to drive at relatively high speed blindfolded through residential Palo Alto areas, while at the same time calling out the color of passing cars, the color of passing homes, and the presence of stop signs. Impressive but not scientific.

That evening at an informal get together at Uri's Palo Alto residence, Geller was able to bend metal rings that were supplied by the SRI researchers, but not without being able to touch them. Upon leaving the residence after that evening of demonstrations, Puthoff and Targ made the following unexpected observation (47):

> As Hal and I walked down Uri's driveway to our
> car, we observed a stop sign quite logically placed
> at the end of the driveway, which intersected a

busy cross street. What was illogical was the unusual condition of the sign, which had been supported by the usual five-foot iron stand. The sign, however, was now only two feet off the ground. That was because its support had been bent and twisted to form three complete loops around an imaginary center of rotation, as if to form a spiral slide about the right size for a mouse. As there was no possibility that we would have missed such an object as we entered Uri's house, the twisting must have occurred during our eight-to-midnight bending session. It was difficult to imagine how such a neat job could have been done without the use of heavy machinery.

An interesting video summary of experiments conducted with Uri Geller by Puthoff and Targ at SRI may be viewed online (52). However, Puthoff and Targ were never able to get Geller to perform a controlled scientific spoon-bending demonstration under remote conditions where Geller did not have any physical contact with the spoon. Yet they were able to observe Geller's ability to modify the weight of an object that was sitting on a precision weighing balance using only the power of his mind. This object was a one gram weight located inside an aluminum can sitting on a balance, and then the whole arrangement covered by a bell jar. Geller's mental efforts produced gains and losses of weight on the order of one gram, which was well outside the noise level of the weight measurements. Puthoff and Targ had no physical explanation as to how Geller might have performed this feat.

Psychokinetic effects and particularly metal bending have been investigated scientifically by the British physicist John Hasted, who has written an entire book about his scientific investigations of this phenomenon (53). Hasted was the head of the experimental physics department at Birkbeck College of the University of London. Interestingly, David Bohm who we have previously discussed for his concepts on wholeness and the implicate order (28) was also a colleague of Hasted's.

Hasted first became aware of the phenomenon of mental metal-bending through the activities of Uri Geller and Geller's association with the Stanford Research Institute. Hasted and Bohm initially met with Geller in February 1974 in London. Since they knew that some people had claimed Geller was simply a very good magician, they took precautions in advance of their meeting. In particular, Hasted brought along with him four of his own brass latchkeys that were quite difficult to bend by hand. Hasted then gave Geller the latchkeys to attempt a metal-bending experiment. Here is his account (53):

> *Geller was quite happy with the keys, and at once took one in each hand, holding it lightly between the forefinger and thumb; I did not take my eyes off them once, not even for a moment. I can affirm that I did not see Geller's other fingers touch the keys (except at pick-up) and that he did not move them more than about an inch from the table surface; they were in my field of vision the whole time. Nothing happened for about forty seconds, and then Geller put the keys flat on the tables about*

> two inches apart and stroked them gently, one
> with each forefinger. All the time Geller was
> talking, but I never took my eyes off the two
> keys and I am certain they never left the table
> for a surreptitious bend to be performed. After
> one more minute's stroking, the end of each key
> started to bend slightly upwards, one (the one
> stroked by his right forefinger) distinctly more
> than the other. The angles were 11 degrees and
> 8 degrees, as measured afterwards.

In another demonstration by Geller, Halsted observed the bending of a metal spoon (53):

> Geller held the handle and did not touch the
> bend. Within a few seconds, and under my
> close scrutiny, the bend in the spoon became
> plastic. It quickly softened so much that the
> spoon could be held with one end in either
> hand and gently moved to and fro. I had
> never seen Geller produce a really plastic bend
> before, and I asked him to hand the spoon to
> me in one piece. . . . . I could sense the plasticity
> myself, by gently moving my hands. It was as
> though the bent part of the spoon was as soft
> as chewing-gum, and yet its appearance was
> normal. . . . . As carefully as I could, I laid it on
> the desk. It was not appreciably warm. I did not
> dare touch the bent part for fear of breaking it,
> and it lay on the desk apparently in one piece
> for a few minutes; but on attempting to move it
> I was unable to prevent it from falling apart, a
> 'neck' having developed.

In this example, Geller was able to bend a piece of molybdenum metal without touching it (53):

> A sudden event observed in an early session of Uri Geller in my laboratory was the bending without touch of a disc-shaped single crystal of molybdenum of about 1 cm diameter. . . . . Physicists David Bohm, Ted Bastin, Jack Sarfatt and also Brendan O'Regan were present as witnesses. . . . . I took the crystal from its box and put it absolutely flat on the plate. Sarfatt extended his hand a few inches above the crystal and the other objects on the plate. Geller moved his hand above Sarfatt's, until a tingling sensation was reported by the latter. Geller tried to 'concentrate his action', and it was suddenly seen by the observers that the crystal had changed its shape, and was now slightly bent, through an angle of about 20 degrees. . . . . But I was absolutely certain that neither Geller nor anyone else had touched the crystal since I placed it on the metal plate; nor did he drop anything on the metal plate.
>
> I replaced the crystal in its box, which I returned to my pocket; a physical examination of the crystal would be necessary. I eventually found that a physical property (the magnetic susceptibility) of the crystal was anomalous. . . . .
>
> Skeptics had a field-day on the basis of this account, and even now it is doubtful if

> *many readers who remember it will be much*
> *influenced by my own version. But I myself*
> *was impressed by what I had seen, and was*
> *reasonably certain that it could not have been*
> *a piece of conjuring. This is partly because*
> *conjurors do no know about how to change the*
> *physical properties of very pure molybdenum;*
> *nor could it have been known just what*
> *investigation I was going to make.*

The metal-bending phenomena that Hasted observed with Geller inspired him to begin an extensive scientific investigation of English children who had also exhibited metal-bending abilities. He employed sensitive scientific equipment to measure and monitor the strains associated with metal bending in real time as they happened. In addition, he did not allow his child metal-benders to touch any of the metal items during his experiments.

At this point I should point out that I am a materials scientist by training and know a good deal about the conditions and mechanisms that are required to permanently bend metals. I will try to describe metal bending in as simplified a description as I can. Take a strip of aluminum metal that is 1/8 inch thick by 1/2 inch wide by 7 inches long and try to bend it using your two hands. What you will do is put your two thumbs underneath the strip and hold the ends of the strip on top with your fingers; then you will exert a bending force on the strip with your hands. This is what materials scientists call "four-point bending". For the dimensions of the aluminum strip specified, most people should be able to bend it at least a little.

Now when the strip is bent, the aluminum metal in the top portion (called the convex surface) stretches in length. It is termed as being in tension. The bottom portion of the strip (called the concave surface) shortens in length and is termed as being in compression. You may ask how the metal can stretch or compress. It does this by the sliding motion of the atomic crystal planes in the metal, a process that is called "dislocation motion" (dislocations are localized re-arrangements of the atomic planes that allow these planes to slide over each other). Atomic crystallographic sliding occurs and the aluminum metal strip forms a bent shape. This process is called plastic deformation bending and has the characteristic that the strip remains bent after you stop applying the force with your hands.

Now what if you try to do the same thing with a strip of steel having the same dimensions? Steel is a much stronger metal than aluminum and, unless you are extremely strong, you will not be able to bend it with your hands even as hard as you may try. You will exert the greatest force that you can, but the steel strip will not permanently bend. It will probably temporarily show a slight springy-type bending, but when you release the force, the strip will become straight again. This process is called elastic bending. You were not able to bend the steel because you could not exert enough force to start the atomic crystal planes sliding one over the other.

The force that you exert on a metal strip depends on the dimensions of the strip, its width, thickness, and length. For a given metal strip of a certain length, the greater its thickness and width, the harder it becomes to permanently bend it. For example, if the 7 inch aluminum strip were

1/4 inch thick and 3/4 inch wide, you would probably not be able to bend it with your hands alone.

Having gone through this simplified description of the metal bending process, we now go back to describe the experiments of Hasted (53).

Hasted placed what are called resistive strain gages on the metal pieces that were to be bent by his child subjects without their touching them. Such gages are just a thin, narrow, long metal strip that is folded into a compact configuration that can be glued onto the metal pieces. When a force is applied to the metal piece, these gages elongate in their length and in doing so change their electrical resistance. This change in electrical resistance can be measured with an electronic circuit and the resistance change related to the amount of change in length of the surface of the metal piece (the "strain" that occurs on its surface). It is a very quantitative and accurate way to measure the elastic strain and the onset of plastic strain in a metal piece that is being subjected to a force.

Remarkably, Hasted's strain gage results established unequivocally that metal pieces were being plastically deformed by his child metal-benders without their touching them in any way. Furthermore, rather than being strictly a bending phenomenon, the strain gage results showed that the deformation appeared to be more like a plastic "churning" of the metal itself, since the measured metal strains were different from those expected during a straightforward bending process. He speculated that the observed deformation phenomena were possibly related to a temporary lowering of the force required to cause the metal to deform by plastic deformation. The yield force of metals can be made to decrease quite dramatically if they are heated. However, Hasted found no evidence that the local temperatures of the metal pieces were elevated, so it did not appear that a localized heating effect was responsible.

In his book, Hasted also described his interactions with French scientists who analyzed the metal-bending abilities of a Parisian by the name of Jean-Pierre Girard. Girard exhibited metal-bending abilities that appear to have been greater than those of Uri Geller. Specifically, Girard was able to deform thick (5/8 inch diameter) round aluminum alloy metal bars that were 10 inches in length. Here is Hasted's description (53):

> *I was present at a session at which Girard was filmed in a deformation requiring 23 Nm; the protocol was good, and, as the video-record shows, the manual force was minimal. It is Girard's custom to hold one end of a bar of circular cross-section in his right hand and pass his left hand slowly over the other end for minutes at a time; he then lays the bar down on a flat surface and rests for a short while. After repeated attempts deformation gradually appears; even a small deformation can be observed if the bar is rolled on a flat surface.*

Girard was hooked up to an EEG machine during the metal bending event. The EEG recorded high levels of alpha waves at a frequency of 10 Hz. Such alpha waves typically occur during relaxation and the onset of sleep, but Girard's recorded heartbeat at the time was 160 beats per minute.

The French research with Girard concentrated on analyzing the metallurgical aspects of paranormal metal-bending. All of the bars bent had their deviations from straightness very accurately measured. The metal microhardness, which is an index of the dislocation structure in the bent metal, was measured at a large number of points in the bar. The residual strain profile in the bar after bending was measured using x-ray diffraction techniques. Bent regions of the bar were analyzed with both scanning and transmission electron microscopy to determine any changes in the metal crystallographic substructure. Electron microprobe analysis was performed to determine the local chemistry of regions of the bar.

The metallurgical analyses indicated that the paranormally bent metal was different from that of normally bent metal. Specifically, the residual stress patterns in the bars bent by Girard were drastically different from those patterns in a normally bent bar. These results suggested that the elastic strain portion of the deformation was essentially eliminated in the paranormally bent bars. It was as if the bars started bending plastically at vary low levels of applied force. This would suggest that significant local softening was occurring at the bent regions by a mechanism other than a localized high temperature, since there was absolutely no evidence of localized temperature increases. It was postulated that large numbers of plastic-deformation-producing dislocations were somehow being produced in the paranormally bent metal and that their subsequent motion to produce deformation was being made abnormally easy by some unknown means. But how such things could happen in the metal was totally unclear to the scientists.

It is evident from the above scientific studies of paranormal metal-bending that the phenomenon of psychokinesis is a real one and not a magic trick. This clearly needs to be explained on some suitable basis, given the controlled and detailed scientific observations that have been made of these effects.

This chapter has been a summary of the various aspects of unexplained reality associated with NDEs, OBEs, ghostly phenomena, and extrasensory perception. To my mind, there is sufficient evidence to indicate that such things are a part of our reality and not something imagined, contrived, mystical, or metaphysical. Even though they do not fit within present scientific paradigms, they still need and deserve to be explained. They cannot be simply discounted from the realm of reality. They are, shall we say, inconvenient truths. Perhaps the scientific paradigms will have to be rewritten in order to encompass them.

Reality of Consciousness

I cannot be totally certain about the reality of the people and things that surround me, but I at least know for sure that I am real. I am conscious that I exist as a real entity. As Descartes most famously and succinctly put it in 1644 "cogito ergo sum" (I think, therefore I am). I have a consciousness that exists and is capable of thought. I know with certainty that I have thoughts and feelings that are my own, that are part of my "inner life". This is a quite basic aspect of reality for every human being.

But just what is this "I" that I am so sure about. There is an interesting article by Deikman that explores the nature of "I" (54). Deikman asks you to consider two experiments. In the first, close your eyes, look inside yourself and try to sense the origin of your most basic, most personal "I". Try to find the root of your "I" feeling. If you do this, you will see that you cannot locate your "I". It eludes you when you try to define it with any action, desire, memory, or thought. What this tells you is that the "I" can be experienced, but it cannot be "seen". Fundamentally, the "I" is the observer, the experiencer that is there prior to any conscious content. Another way to express this is that the "I" is identically equal to awareness.

In the next experiment, consider that you are in a sensory deprivation chamber. It is totally dark and completely silent. Your body is floating in a warm liquid, so you have no sensory touch inputs. There are no smells and no tastes. Your five senses are completely shut down. In this state, you are totally isolated from the outside world. The only things that you have are your thoughts and feelings. However, even these mental states come and go. But the one thing that remains is your awareness—your awareness is your "I".

Is your "I", your awareness, produced simply by material brain function, or is it something else entirely? Every night during your non-REM sleep, your "I" seems to disappear, only to reappear during REM sleep and when you awake. If someone knocks you unconscious, your conscious "I" disappears temporarily until you regain consciousness. The same is true if you are anesthetized. So clearly brain function is a necessary condition for a conscious "I". However a central question is whether the "I" also exists when your brain is unconscious.

What is the reality of my own personal consciousness? Where does my consciousness reside and what is its nature? My personal experience is that my consciousness seems to reside in my head, somewhere just behind my eyes. The head is a logical place to perceive consciousness. After all, it is the site of the brain as well as four of the five senses. So it seems reasonable that I would locate my consciousness there rather then someplace else in my body, say my knee for example.

What goes on with my consciousness during a typical day of my current lifestyle (you might also call this a day in the life of "I")? The first thing that happens is that I wake up from the night's sleep. For a short period of time, I may remember some aspects about the dream I was dreaming just before waking. The need to perform certain bodily functions rises into my consciousness, but only when their call becomes somewhat urgent. Actually, I have little awareness of most of my body functions unless I choose to focus on them. Moving my head and my limbs, breathing, blinking my eyes are all relatively automatic.

During the day, legions of thoughts pass through my head. Some are mundane and regular. I need to take the dog out when he comes in proximity with his "I really must go" little whine. In the morning when I first take him for his walk, I feel the cool breeze and breathe the fresh morning air. I see the sun about to rise and marvel at the magnificence of the morning sky. My vision takes in the plants, flowers, and shrubs that surround our dwelling place.

I make myself breakfast and then have a cup of coffee while I sit down at my computer and review the emails that have accumulated during the night. My thoughts are centered on them and on the news that I review through my computer screen. I think about the things I want to try and accomplish during the new day.

My wife wakes up and we exchange morning pleasantries. I go and perform the rituals of making our bed and shaving and washing my face, while my wife bustles around with her morning chores.

Then I go back to my computer and begin performing my intellectual work of the day. At the present moment, this involves thinking about the content of the book that I am writing, and then trying to express my thoughts in a semi-coherent way. Other days it may involve other intellectual pursuits. My thoughts roam around the ideas and concepts that I wish to convey in my book. This may also involve searches on the computer for information that is related to the concepts that I am attempting to formulate and shape in my mind. My thoughts are of a much more abstract character than my everyday thoughts, as you can easily see by reading what I have written to try and understand the nature of reality.

At various times during the day, my consciousness becomes occupied with more mundane, analytical things. I have bills to pay and chores to do. Since I am a scientist, part of my time is devoted to attempting to stay current with the latest new developments that are happening in the realm of science. I track and read scientific journals on a daily basis.

During an average day, my consciousness often dwells on memories both recent and from long ago. Recent memories are near-term things such as "when did I last take the dog out" or "when will my wife return from her errands". But the long-term memories are another matter. When I drift into these memories, it is truly amazing to me how much I can remember from such long ago times. I can remember minute details of places and events that happened when I was a child. I see again in my mind the layout of both the interior and exterior of the home where I first lived more than 50 years ago. It all comes back so vividly. How do these memories enter into my consciousness, and from where?

In any given day, events perturb my consciousness from the outside world which are completely unexpected and unanticipated. The phone rings and I need to take some action based upon the call. Or I run into a person and have an unexpected interaction with them. It seems that such things enter my consciousness from outside my "inner space". They are happening because something external to me produced them. What is the nature of that externalness?

Sometime every day I spend time in meditation. This is an activity that I have been doing for many years and I must say that I believe it has had a positive influence on expanding the level of my consciousness. To enter the meditative state, I sit in a chair in a quiet place, close my eyes, and then go through a mental procedure that is designed to clear my mind of all the thoughts that it normally has. When I achieve the non-thought state (which I am now able to do during most of my meditative sessions thanks to years of practice) my consciousness essentially "blanks out". This state has a resemblance to non-REM sleep but it differs in that I still seem to retain a sense of awareness, but it is awareness without thought; I am quite certain that I am not asleep. After a period of time, typically 30-40 minutes, my thoughts will return spontaneously and I come out of deep meditation. During the time I am in it, I have absolutely no memory of where "I" was and what "I" was doing. Where was my consciousness during meditation?

Each day there are moments when I experience personal qualia, my subjective consciousness experiences. For example, the calendar on my wall is currently showing a photo of a beautiful red flower with a magnificent dragonfly sitting on it. These miracles of nature inspire me. I seem to have inherited an eye for art somewhere, even though I have trouble making even simple drawings on my own. I look up and see the painting of an island landscape that my daughter painted when she was a child and it delights my eye, as do the pastel paintings that my artistically gifted wife produces.

I try and get some rigorous physical exercise almost every day because I spend a lot of time sitting in a chair at my computer and I need to make up for this. Sometimes I use the cross-country ski machine that sits out on my balcony, sometimes I go down to the exercise room in our condo building and use the treadmill or stationary bike, and sometimes my wife and I go for long walks on the beautiful beach that is not far from our home. Except for the beach walks, I listen to music when I exercise. The music resonates with my consciousness, takes my mind away from the exercise routine, and makes me feel happy.

In the evenings I have dinner and conversation with my wife and then retire again into my study for another session of intellectual pursuits. The computer and internet have been a great aid to me in terms of expanding my personal consciousness into very many areas. I am a voracious reader and the bookshelf in my study is crammed to overflowing with books. I seek out books on spirituality, consciousness, roots of religions, the paranormal, and the mysterious and unexplained.

Before retiring for the evening, I typically watch something on television to mentally relax. Then I climb into bed and apply a meditative technique to fall asleep quickly. During the cycles of my non-REM sleep, I have absolutely no memory of what may or may not have taken place, or of my awareness. In the cycles of REM sleep, I have dreams where I am one of the characters in the dream action, and these dreams often incorporate elements of my conscious memory. Then I wake up the next morning and the next day in the life of my consciousness begins.

The reason that I have gone through this perhaps slightly tedious description of a day's worth of my consciousness is not to bore you but rather to illustrate the very subjective nature of consciousness. These are some of the thoughts and feelings, the qualia, which are associated with my consciousness every day. They certainly appear to be unique personal thoughts and experiences that seem almost impossible for a chemical biological machine to produce. The question is how do they occur?

At the present time, many of the people who investigate the nature of consciousness are of the opinion that there are two aspects to it. These are termed access consciousness and phenomenal consciousness. Access consciousness is associated with information in our minds that is accessible for verbal reporting, reasoning, and the control of behavior. This is the more mechanistic aspect of consciousness that is generally termed the "easy problem of consciousness" and is thought to be associated with brain mechanisms.

But then there is phenomenal consciousness. It is the subjective aspect of consciousness associated with the subjective "qualia" that we all experience, such as the things I described in my day in the life. Phenomenal consciousness is described as the "hard problem of consciousness" because it is much harder to conceive how it occurs.

The term "hard problem of consciousness" was coined by consciousness researcher David Chalmers at a famous meeting on the subject held in Tucson, Arizona in 1994 (55). It is essentially this: How do physical processes in the brain produce subjective experiences? In other words, how are the first-person "I" experiences (i.e. qualia) produced by third-person brain events. Chalmers formulation of the "hard problem" has defined intellectual discussions of consciousness since he first put it forward in 1994.

The people who study consciousness fall into two camps. The first group seeks solutions through materialist explanations of brain function for both access and phenomenal aspects. We will call this group the "consciousness monists". The second group thinks that while access consciousness is related to brain function, phenomenal consciousness involves something more than just brain material, something much less tangible than the mass of neurons in the brain. This group we term the "consciousness dualists".

Consciousness monists say that we are nothing more than body and brain. Our consciousness is essentially a result of brain function. They argue that there is no such thing as spirit or soul. The most famous recent monist has been Francis Crick, the Nobel Prize winner for the discovery of the structure of DNA. Crick put forward the "astonishing hypothesis". Basically, the "astonishing hypothesis" says (as expressed by Crick) *"that 'you', your joys and your sorrows, your memories and your ambitions, your sense of personal identity and free will, are in fact no more than the behavior of a vast assembly of nerve cells and their associated molecules"*. In other words, your consciousness is essentially the integrated activities of your nerve and brain cells. The central problem with the monist approach is that no one has yet been able to scientifically determine where or how brain cells and their associated brain centers integrate the consciousness. One cannot identify where in the brain the consciousness is located or how consciousness is assembled in the brain. Nor can monists effectively explain the subjective "I" qualia.

There are two general monist concepts of the brain and consciousness. The first suggests that specific groups of neurons in the brain are associated with specific conscious experiences. That was Crick's view. This concept surmises that there is one set of brain neuron groupings for, say, the conscious experience of the beauty of a painting, and another different set of neuron groups for, say, the conscious idea of God. The second approach conceives that consciousness is derived from a more generalized increase in the brain's neural activity. However this view says nothing about what creates consciousness in the brain, but only what controls the level of consciousness. The first approach might be described as the "neuron quality" viewpoint, while the second as the "neuron quantity" concept.

Consciousness dualists, on the other hand, argue that first-person "I" experiences such as qualia are associated with a mind function that is somehow separate from just the materialistic firing of collections of neurons in the brain, but which controls the patterns of neuron firing in some subtle way. David Chalmers, who first brought the "hard problem" to the forefront is the most prominent current consciousness dualist.

The most famous early consciousness dualist was Rene Descartes, the discoverer of the Cartesian coordinate system. Descartes said the body and the spirit (soul) coexist together in the living person. It is the spirit that is the conscious entity and that embodies the mind. Descartes' concept is termed "the ghost in the machine". The body and the brain are physical entities, while the spirit and mind are spiritual entities. Thus, they are fundamentally different from each other and this raises the key scientific problem with the "ghost in the machine", which is: How does the "ghost" interface with the "machine"? This is certainly a very valid scientific question. How do our sensory inputs from the physical world outside get to the spirit, the mind, so that the mind can think about them and feel them? Similarly, how do the thoughts and decisions generated by the mind translate into actual physical actions? Descartes postulated that this interfacing took place in the pineal gland at the center of the brain.

Present day consciousness dualists reject Descartes' spiritual explanation of consciousness in favor of more scientifically-based approaches, many of them associated with the mysteries inherent in quantum mechanics that I have previously described. They seek a quantum mechanical mechanism that can couple to the mechanics of brain cell functioning to provide explanations for the subjective functioning of the mind.

The various views of these two consciousness groups have been very nicely summarized in a book by Susan Blackmore (56). In it, Blackmore conducted interviews with twenty prominent philosophers and scientists who have been studying consciousness in depth. She herself has done considerable work in this area and must certainly be considered a group member. She would probably classify herself as a consciousness monist, but one with underlying, nagging doubts and a fondness for Buddhist concepts.

Blackmore formulated a list of standardized questions about consciousness to pose to each of her interviewees. The first question was: What is the problem? In other words, why is consciousness such a difficult subject to get one's hands around as compared to other scientific subjects? This question was posed to try and define the difficulties with consciousness, and also to have the interviewees identify themselves with either the monist or the dualist consciousness groups.

Blackmore also asked the interviewees for their views about "zombies". In the consciousness community, the topic of zombies revolves around the following thought experiment. Is it possible for there to be a being who looks exactly like you and responds exactly like you in terms of speech, externally expressed thoughts, and external actions, but who has no inner, subjective life?

Another of Blackmore's questions was: Do you believe in life after death? Blackmore herself felt that a personal life after death would be incompatible with a scientific view of the world. She was interesting in knowing what the other interviewees thought about this, probably to compare their responses to her own monist view. Clearly, monists would answer in the negative, while dualists would be more open to the possibility.

All the above questions that Blackmore presented to her interviewees have an important bearing on the issues associated with the reality of consciousness. I will now elaborate on a few of the responses that she received, starting with the monists.

Blackmore interviewed the monist Francis Crick shortly before his death in 2004. When Blackmore asked Crick why consciousness was such a difficult problem, he replied (56):

> *There's no easy way of explaining consciousness in terms of known science. The easiest way to talk about the problem is in terms of qualia. For example—how can you explain the redness of red in terms of physics and chemistry?*

Crick agreed that the hard problem was the crux of the difficulty in understanding consciousness. He went on to indicate that he was looking for brain neural correlates that correspond to what we are conscious of. Particularly, he was seeking to determine the difference in brain activity when a person was conscious as compared to when they were unconscious. In other words, he wanted to establish the brain mechanisms for the unconscious mind in the hope that this would reveal a materialist source of qualia. But one got the clear impression from his interview that he did not have a rationale for where in the brain to even begin looking.

Then there was the interview with the well-known monist Daniel Dennett. Dennett is a professor of philosophy at Tufts University in Massachusetts and director of the Center for Cognitive Studies there. He is also the author of the well-read book with the audacious title "Consciousness Explained". He takes the position that there is no hard problem, that qualia simply do not exist, that they are actually a delusion that people experience for reasons that are unclear. When Dennett expresses the "I" word, he takes it to relate to the "agent" that he argues is the whole body of an individual. Oddly enough, Dennett expressed the view that he, the "agent", had a free will (56):

> The model that we want to have for free will is of an agent that is autonomous, not in some metaphysical sense, but in the sense of being able to act on the reasons that matter to the agent, and who's got the information that is needed to act in a timely fashion.

The problem I have with Dennett is that he is a philosopher and not a scientist like Crick. There seems no phenomenological basis for his rejection of the existence of qualia, which I unequivocally know I have. I am in no way delusional when I experience them, they seem fundamental to me. But then, as Dennett stated: *"Philosophy is what you do when you don't yet know what the right questions are to ask"*.

Now let us see what a few dualists have to say about consciousness. We begin with David Chalmers, the person who coined the term "the hard problem" in 1994. Chalmers was born in Australia in 1966. He first began studying mathematics but then became fascinated with the topic of consciousness and earned a Ph.D in philosophy and cognitive science from Indiana University. Following a number of years as Director of the Center for Consciousness Studies at the University of Arizona, he then returned to Australia to take the position of Director for Consciousness Studies at the Australian National University. Here is how Chalmers described the hard problem in his conversation with Susan Blackmore (56):

> *The heart of the science of consciousness is trying to understand the first person perspective. When we look at the world from the perspective of science, we take the third person perspective. We see a subject as a body with a brain, and with certain behaviour. We can be terribly objective, but something very important about being a human being is left out. As human beings we all know that it feels like something, from the inside. We have sensations, thoughts, and feelings. . . . . The hard problem is the question of explaining how*

> *it is that all this is accompanied by subjective experience. That seems to go beyond any mechanistic question about how the various behaviours and functions are produced.*

Interestingly, Chalmers stated that he agreed with Descartes' famous statement about consciousness, *cogito ergo sum* (I think, therefore I am). For Chalmers, dealing with the subjective nature of consciousness requires a paradigm shift. He believes that consciousness must be treated as a fundamental of nature, along with other fundamentals of nature such as energy, charge, and spin. Only by taking such an approach can a bridge be built between the third-person science of brain function and the first-person nature of consciousness.

When Chalmers was asked if he believed in free will, his response was that he didn't know what free will meant. And when questioned about what happens to consciousness after death, he said that he would probably cease to exist, but it would be very nice if he were completely wrong about this.

Roger Penrose and Stuart Hameroff have coupled their respective areas of expertise in an attempt to develop a scientific basis for Chalmers' view of consciousness as a fundamental aspect of nature. Penrose is a professor of mathematics at the University of Oxford. He was knighted for his contributions to science, and is well-known for his 1989 book "The Emperor's New Mind" which suggested links between consciousness and quantum mechanics. Hameroff is an anesthesiologist, a medical field closely associated with human consciousness. He is a professor of Anesthesiology and Psychology at the University of Arizona.

Penrose feels that the link between science and the hard problem of consciousness lies in the area of quantum mechanics. Perhaps the reason for his feeling is that both quantum mechanics and consciousness subjectivity are, at their root, "strange" in the sense that they seem to transcend physical reality as we currently understand it. Being a mathematician, he bases his belief on Godel's famous incompleteness theory of mathematic logic as follows (56):

> I'm saying that the Godel argument tells us that we are not simply computational entities; that our understanding is something outside computation. It doesn't tell us it's something unphysical, but there's a crucial thing that's missing, which has to do with quantum mechanics. . . . . Quantum mechanics is the most obvious place where we don't know enough about physics. Where do you see non-computability in physics? You don't seem to see it anywhere else. So this, therefore, is presumably where it is.

Having made the assumption that the essence of consciousness lies in quantum mechanics, the next scientific step is to try and establish a link between quantum mechanics and brain mechanisms. This is where Hameroff's expertise comes in. Hameroff has been studying protein structures called microtubules in the internal structure of brain cells. It is in the biochemistry of the tiny microtubules that he thinks quantum mechanics might have the possibility of influencing brain mechanics.

Blackmore asked Hameroff what he thought happens to consciousness after death and this was his response (56):

> *When the quantum coherence in the microtubules is lost, as in cardiac arrest, or death, the Planck scale quantum information in our heads dissipates, leaks out, to the Planck scale in the universe as a whole. The quantum information which had comprised our conscious and subconscious minds during life doesn't completely dissipate, but hangs together because of quantum entanglement. Because it stays in quantum superposition and doesn't undergo quantum state reduction or collapse, it's more like our subconscious mind, like our dreams. And because the universe at the Planck scale is non-local, it exists holographically, indefinitely. Is this the soul? Why not.*

So there you have an encapsulation of the views of a few of the current leading lights on the subject of consciousness, both monists and dualists. Into which camp does your intuition take you? Consciousness is indeed the hardest of hard problems.

We will end this discussion of the reality of consciousness by saying a bit about the Global Consciousness Project.

The predecessor of the Global Consciousness Project was the Princeton Engineering Anomalies Research (PEAR) program at Princeton University. One of the primary areas of research was to determine if human consciousness could influence random number generators. A random number generator is an electronic device that generates a random sequence of numbers; the simplest to generate is just a random sequence of the binary numbers 0 and 1. If one has a random sequence of 0's and 1's, the mean value of a large sequence will be ½ because just about as many 0's will come up as do 1's if a large enough sample is taken. This is the electronic equivalent of randomly flipping a coin and measuring the occurrence of heads or tails, except that it is much more truly random than any physical coin flipping experiment.

The PEAR program demonstrated with high statistical significance that a human being could use their consciousness to "will" the appearance of more 1's than 0's, or more 0's than 1's in a sequence of binary bits (57). The effect was however small, of the order of 0.0005 per binary bit. That is to say, if one had a random sequence of 100,000 binary bits, you would normally expect 50,000 of them to be 0's and 50,000 of them to be 1's. However, when people tried to "will" say more 1's to occur, then the observation was that the random number generator produced 50,050 of the 1's. This was a small but statistically quite significant effect that could be produced by one human being acting alone with their consciousness.

The Global Consciousness Project was begun in 1998 to determine if much larger numbers of people could have more of an effect on a random number generation scheme that was global in nature. To this end, over 60 sophisticated random number generators (RNGs) are located at the present time in diverse locations around the globe. There are presently RNGs sited in Europe, the US, Canada, India, Fiji, New Zealand, Japan, China, Russia, Brazil, Africa, Thailand, South America, and Australia. These RNGs generate binary random number sequences (0's and 1's) through the completely random process of quantum tunneling in an electronic device. There can be no doubt that the RNGs are producing truly random binary number sequences in the absence of any external physical influence, since significant protections are in place to isolate these devices from any external electronic effects. The RNGs run around the clock and transmit their data via the internet to a central collection point. At this collection point, the data are analyzed to determine if there are any deviations from global randomness at any given point in time.

The central hypothesis of the Global Consciousness Project is the following (58):

> *Periods of collective emotional or attentional behavior in widely distributed populations will correlate with deviations from expectation in a global network of RNGs.*

Thus, the investigation seeks to correlate global randomness with high-impact, high visibility events that occur from time-to-time in the world. 390 such events have been evaluated as of the year 2011. Some of these events are:

> U.S. Embassy bombings in Africa on August 7, 1998
> JFK Jr. death on July 17, 1999

Millennium Event on January 1, 2000

Terrorist attacks on September 11, 2001

9/11 one year anniversary on September 11, 2002

Columbia space shuttle disaster on February 1, 2003

Catastrophic tsunami on December 26, 2004

Hurricane Katrina landfall in New Orleans on August 29, 2005

Saddam Hussein's execution on December 30, 2006

Benizar Bhutto assassination on December 27, 2007

Chinese earthquake on May 12, 2008.

President Barack Obama inauguration on January 20, 2009

Earthquake in Haiti on January 12, 2010

Osama Bin Laden killed on May 2, 2011

Let's describe the Global Consciousness Project results for one particularly traumatic worldwide event, the September 11, 2001 terrorist attacks on New York and Washington DC (59). The measurement of global non-randomness began to become significant about one hour after the collapse of the second World Trade Center building. Presumably this was the time that the maximum level of global awareness and concern took hold. The global non-randomness then continued at a high level until September 16, when the published analysis of the data was terminated. The probability that the measured level of global non-randomness on September 11 was an actual, true phenomenon was determined to be 99.95% through a rigorous statistical evaluation of the global RNG data.

As of the year 2011, the cumulative global non-randomness data obtained by the Global Consciousness Project for the 390 global events analyzed thus far have shown that this is a real effect to a probability of 99.999999999%. Clearly the effect is real. What is completely missing is a scientific explanation for the observed phenomenon. Right now there is absolutely no explanation as to how a global awareness/consciousness of a major global event can have such a dramatic non-randomness effect on the electronic generation of world-wide random number generators which, according should to our current scientific paradigms, should be producing absolutely random numbers.

The material presented in this chapter should make it clear to you how little we know about the nature of consciousness. We definitely know that we are conscious beings, but we do not know how consciousness is formulated in the brain, nor do we have a clue how objective brain mechanics produce subjective feelings and emotions, the "qualia" that constitute our inner self. Consciousness is far-and-away the number one "Mystery of the Mind". And I believe it is the key to unlocking knowledge and understanding of the true nature of reality.

A Larger Reality

I would like to preface the discussion in this chapter by saying that major elements of it rely on my own personal intuition. I cannot "prove" in an experimentally-based scientific manner that they are correct. No one can at this specific moment of human development. I simply ask that you reflect upon them in the light of your own intuitive feelings.

Most present day scientists and intellectuals are firmly rooted in the Physical Reality Framework. For them, only what we can detect with our physical senses or the scientific instruments that are an extension of them is the fabric of reality. Reality must fit comfortably within the theoretical formalisms of materialist philosophy and science. Yet we have shown in this book that there are many phenomena that seem to lie outside of the lexicon of the physical reality worldview. Such phenomena are either dismissed out-of-hand as superstition or delusion, or simply ignored as if they did not exist. But we can no longer dismiss or ignore these phenomena. They do exist as a part of our reality and they must be incorporated into our view of reality if we are to understand what is truly real.

The Physical Reality Framework puts its stock in reality on the immutable basis of what's "out there". But what do we know of the outside physical world really? The philosopher Immanuel Kant was the first to address this question head-on. Kant (1724-1804) separated observations into the "noumenon" and the "phenomenon". The noumenon is taken to be the "thing in itself" and the phenomenon is the thing as it appears to an observer. Kant argued that the noumenon cannot really be known by the observer. The only thing the observer can know is the appearance of the noumenon in his mind, the phenomenon.

Let us make Kant's philosophical statement more concrete by applying it to what we see when we look at a red rose flower. When we observe a rose with our eyes, we see its shape and form and the context of the things that are immediately around it, such as its stem. Our color vision also tells us that the rose is red in color. These are the things that we think we know when we see a red rose. If we used another of our senses, we could also smell the fragrance of the rose, but I will neglect the other senses and focus only on sight in this example, since much is known about the physical, biological, and, to a much lesser extent, neurological aspects of seeing something with our eyes.

As we look at the red rose, light reflected from the flower enters both our eyes through the eye lens of each eye. One should note that it is only the light rays reflected from the surface of the rose that reach our eyes. A red rose appears red because it reflects the red portion of the visible light spectrum, while absorbing the other spectrum colors. This reflected light from the surface of the rose then strikes the retina, the back surface of the eye, forming an inverted image of the rose there. The image is inverted due to the bending of light rays in the eye lens.

The retina contains an array of cells on its surface that produce electrical signals when struck by light rays. There are two types of cells, rod cells and cone cells. The rod cells are spread over a larger portion of the retina than are the cone cells. Rod cells are only sensitive to the colors black and white but their light sensitivity is greater than that of cone cells. The rod cells allow a person to see things in dim light conditions. Cone cells can discriminate between the different wavelengths of the incoming light, but they are less sensitive to light intensity in comparison to the rod cells. For this reason, they tend to be concentrated in the retina close to the position of the lens and near the optic nerve. This is the reason why colors are less intense in a person's peripheral vision.

Cone cells can discriminate between three different wavelength ranges of light centered roughly around the colors red, green, and blue. These three colors are called the primary colors, since all the other colors can be derived through appropriate combinations of them. There are three types of cone retinal cells, small wavelength S cells (maximum sensitivity at 440 nanometer blue light), medium wavelength M cells (maximum sensitivity at 540 nanometer green light), and long wavelength L cells (maximum sensitivity at 580 nanometer red light). Using a combination of these cells, the human eye can detect color wavelengths in the range of 400-700 nanometers (dark blue to dark red).

When the reflected red light from the red rose enters the eye, it activates just the M and L retinal cones since the red light falls out of the range of the S cones. What do we mean by activate? In the retina, the cone photoreceptor cells send electrical signals to lower-down bipolar cells that in turn send other electrical signals to even further-down ganglion cells, which then send electrical signals to the brain via the optic nerve. Experiments have shown that approximately 9000 kilobits per second of electrical visual information can be transmitted to the brain by the action of the retinal cells. The brain receives this information in a time of the order of 50 milliseconds.

The optic nerves from each eye travel into the brain and cross at an area called the optic chiasma. Once this crossing takes place, electrical signals from the left eye proceed to the right occipital lobe at the back of the brain, and signals from the right eye are routed to the left occipital lobe. It is interesting that the optical processing areas of the brain are located at the back of the brain, far away from the source of the signals at the eye retinas.

Image creation happens at the right and left occipital lobes in the back of the brain. This is where the magic takes place. No neuroscientist really knows how the brain constructs the image from the influx of electrical signals that it is receiving. The perceived image of the red rose, its size, shape, three-dimensional character, and color are somehow composed by the brain into a coherent whole image. With regard to the color of the rose, it will never be a pure spectral wavelength, but rather a combination based upon the mix of primary colors that are being received, including those of the background elements associated with the rose. There are almost an infinite number of such combinations which can produce something that a person would call red in color.

The terminology "the redness of red" is used as an example of a qualium by the people who think about the "hard problem" of consciousness. To the individual consciousness, the redness perceived through the action of brain processes has a certain "feel" to it that is highly subjective in nature. As the renowned scientist Erwin Schroedinger (who formulated the most important equation in quantum mechanics) put it (60):

> *The sensation of colour cannot be accounted for by the physicist's objective picture of light-waves. Could the physiologist account for it, if he had fuller knowledge than he has of the processes in the retina and the nervous processes set up by them in the optical nerve bundles and in the brain? I do not think so.*

The red rose that one sees with the eyes could be a vibrant red, or perhaps only a dull red. It could be a mild red or an intense red. It could be a red that makes you happy or a red that makes you sad. These things are all a part of the "redness of red".

I experience some of my personal qualia when I go to art museums, something I very much enjoy doing. Although I can only make the most rudimentary of drawings myself, for some unknown reason I seem to have an excellent eye for fine art. Take for example the very famous painting by Botticelli "The Birth of Venus", which I had the opportunity to view up close and personal during a visit to the Uffizi Museum in Florence, Italy. The most striking thing about this painting to my mind is the face and hair. Her face and hair are extremely pleasing to my eye. That is the best way I can describe it. The face is so serene and her auburn hair is an amazing flow of fine tendrils. I try to imagine who she was in real life. This is an example of one of my qualia, my "feeling" for fine art.

How do physical processes in the brain produce these highly subjective feelings that I experience when I view "The Birth of Venus". I agree with Erwin Schroedinger. Such subjectivity cannot be a product of brain neurochemistry.

Let us take an even deeper step into the Physical Reality Framework and consider what physicists call the "fundamentals" of nature. These fundamentals are physical quantities that cannot be described as combinations of other physical quantities. Such fundamentals apply to all of the physical "stuff" in the universe. The fundamentals of nature as conceived by our present science are the following: Spacetime, Energy, Charge, and Spin. All of these fundamentals came into existence at the event of the Big Bang which is thought to have taken place 13.7 billion years ago when "Everything" popped out in a single point from "Nothing".

Spacetime is the framework in which all the physical "stuff" in the universe exists. It is conceived as a continuum, meaning that it changes smoothly from point-to-point. Each point in spacetime is characterized by three dimensional coordinates and one time coordinate. Spacetime is the basis of Einstein's theory of relativity. Prior to Einstein, the framework for everything was thought to be the "ether". The "ether" was considered to be an "ethereal" substance of fundamental composition in which everything existed and an absolute frame of reference. It was also the medium through which light propagated and the speed of light was thus thought to be dictated by the properties of the "ether". However, the famous Michelson-Morley experiment of 1887 showed conclusively that the "ether" did not exist and so paved the way for Einstein's relativity theory. A fundamental aspect of Einstein's theory of relativity and spacetime is that the speed of light is a constant relative to any two observers moving with respect to each other.

Energy is the next fundamental. Physics textbooks will tell you that the definition of energy is "the ability to do work". However, this is not a very satisfying definition because it states what energy does, but not what energy is. In fact, no one really knows what the essence of energy is. There are many different forms of energy such as kinetic energy, potential energy, heat energy, electrical energy, electromagnetic energy, and also physical matter. For unknown reasons, it is a law of nature that energy is never created or destroyed when it changes form, it is always conserved.

Physical matter is just a form of "condensed energy". All matter has a quantity called "mass". What is mass? The most basic way to define it is as the "rest (or invariant) mass". The rest mass of matter is related to the energy contained in the matter by Einstein's famous equation E =

mc^2, where c is the speed of light in a pure vacuum. This relationship shows that mass and energy are fundamentally the same. In a nuclear bomb, a small amount of mass is converted into a tremendous amount of energy because the speed of light is such a large number. In a nuclear accelerator, the energy of two protons colliding can be converted into a very small mass of subatomic particles. In his theory of general relativity, Einstein showed that the presence of large amounts of mass can warp the fabric of spacetime, thus producing the apparent force of gravity. Although all matter has mass, photons of electromagnetic radiation such as visible light have no mass. They are massless entities. Despite being massless, photons do possess energy through the famous Planck equation $E = h\nu$, where ν is the frequency of the photon radiation and h is a fundamental constant called Planck's constant.

Charge is another fundamental of nature. Charge is a property of matter that causes the matter to experience a force when in the presence of other pieces of matter than contain charge. Charge comes in elementary units that are given the symbol "e", and can be either positive or negative. Charged particles of the same sign repel each other, while charged particles of opposite signs attract one another. The charge on a proton in the nucleus of an atom is +1, while that of an electron in an atom is -1. Even subatomic particles such as quarks possess charge but in these cases the charges are less than 1 (either -1/3 or +2/3). Unlike matter, photons of radiation such as visible light have a zero charge.

The last fundamental of physics is spin. When one hears the word "spin", one thinks of some object that is undergoing a circular angular motion around a stationary axis that is perpendicular to the plane of the spinning object. A child's top spins, an airplane propeller spins, the Earth spins around its axis. This type of spin is called angular momentum. The basic particles of matter also have "spin", but in this case it is quite difficult to define any actual spinning motion of these particles. Electrons, protons, and neutrons all have a "spin" which, in this case, is not continuous but comes in specific, quantized amounts. The spin of these particles can be either one of two states, the states of "spin up" or "spin down". In terms of the magnitude of the spin (which has units of energy multiplied by time), the spin of these basic particles is given by $S = h/4\pi$, where h is Planck's constant. Photons also have a "spin up" and "spin down" characteristic, where the spin axis is the direction of motion of the photon. For a photon the spin is given by $S = h/2\pi$, so the photon spin is twice that of the electron. For the case of photons, spin is associated with photon polarization.

So there you have a brief (and as non-technical as I can make it) summary of the "fundamentals" of our current physics. These fundamentals form the basis of the present scientific explanation of physical reality. As you may have noticed, the fundamentals themselves are just "there" because they allow the current scientific theories to explain the results obtained from scientific experiments. However, they are themselves essentially metaphysical, because we can go no further in understanding the "why" of them with our present science.

However, in the previous chapters of this book, I have outlined a body of observations that do not fit within the present Physical Reality Framework. These include the veridical aspects reported during near-death experiences, out-of-body experiences, the reports of ghostly phenomena, clairvoyance, telekinesis, the placebo effect, and global focus effects on random number generation. None of these things fit into the Physical Reality Framework of our current science, and so there are only two options for scientists. The first is to dismiss all of these observations as being unreal for one reason or another. But the second option is to entertain the possibility that the Physical Reality Framework is deficient, and thus requires either significant modifications or the introduction of a new, more expansive, framework.

If we look at the science of cosmology, we see that the present thinking is that our entire physical universe came into existence 13.7 billion years ago in the emergence of all energy and matter instantaneously from a single point that originated essentially from "nothing". This Big Bang produced all the "stuff" and also all the fundamentals and laws of physics that we currently know. But as to what caused the Big Bang and where all the stuff and fundamentals came from, we are at a complete loss to explain it in terms of any scientific theory that can be experimentally tested and verified.

In a similar vein, the current theory of quantum mechanics says that reality is produced by the act of observation. Quantum mechanics posits that there is no underlying reality until there is an observed reality. Not only is this position intuitively disturbing, it also obviously begs the question: Who is the observer?

For materialists, it is an inconvenient truth that for the human understanding of reality to progress, there must be a new Framework developed that is able to encompass the many and varied aspects of reality that have been observed in actual fact. In this regard, it seems clear that the fundamental which is missing from the current Physical Reality Framework is—Consciousness.

The new paradigm that I espouse based upon what I know and what I intuit is the Universal Consciousness Framework. This cannot really be considered a "new" paradigm, since major elements of it are contained in the ancient teachings of India. However, it is a significant departure from the thinking of those in so-called developed societies. What I will do now is to attempt to flesh out and expound upon some of the aspects of this new Framework.

The basic premise of the Universal Consciousness Framework is that all reality derives from a non-physical Universal Consciousness which is the only true Fundamental that exists. This Universal Consciousness is non-physical in that it resides somewhere outside our physical reality, the physical universe that we can detect with our senses and our scientific instruments. However, the non-physical Universal Consciousness is the source of everything in the physical reality.

What can we, as physical human beings, know of this Universal Consciousness? Well, we can start with our personal consciousness. We know that we are conscious beings who are aware of our existence. So our personal consciousness equals personal awareness. And what is awareness? Awareness is the ability to experience "being". From this, it seems logical to assume that Universal Consciousness equals Universal Awareness.

There are very few people who have felt they had an experience of Universal Consciousness. One of these people is Richard Maurice Bucke. Bucke was a Canadian physician and psychiatrist who had an overwhelming consciousness experience in 1872. Since Bucke considered himself to be a man of logic, he chose to write his account in the third person to express its factuality and accuracy (61):

> It was in the early spring at the beginning of his thirty-sixth year. He and two friends had spent the evening reading Wordsworth, Shelley, Keats, Browning, and especially Whitman. They parted at midnight, and he had a long drive in a hansom (it was in an English city). His mind, deeply under the influences of the ideas, images, and emotions called up by the reading and talk of the evening, was calm and peaceful. He was in a state of quiet, almost passive enjoyment. All at once, without warning of any kind, he found himself wrapped around, as it were, by a flame-colored cloud. For an instant he thought of fire, some sudden conflagration in the great city; the next he knew that the light was within himself.

> Directly afterwards came upon him a sense of exultation, of immense joyousness, accompanied or immediately followed by an intellectual illumination quite impossible

to describe. Into his brain streamed one momentary lightning flash of the Brahmic Splendor which has ever since lightened his life; upon his heart fell one drop of Brahmic Bliss, leaving thenceforward for always an aftertaste of heaven. Among other things he did come to believe, he saw and knew that the Cosmos is not dead matter but a living Presence, that the soul of man is immortal, that the universe is so built and ordered that without any peradventure, all things work together for the good of each and all, that the foundation principle of the world is what we call love and that the happiness of everyone is, in the long run, absolutely certain. He claims that he learned more within the few seconds during which the illumination lasted than in previous months or even years of study and that he learned much that no study could ever have taught.

During his experience, Bucke was shown that there is a loving Cosmic Presence, that we have an immortal soul, and that *"the happiness of everyone is, in the long run, absolutely certain".* As a result of his experience, Bucke coined the term "Cosmic Consciousness", a phrase that I must say resonates with me on a deep level. Cosmic Consciousness is another name for Universal Consciousness.

The Universal Consciousness is non-physical. What does that mean? One thing it might mean is that Universal Consciousness exists in a higher dimensional plane than our three-dimensional physical plane.

We live in a three-dimensional world, with time as a fourth non-spatial dimension. That's the observable fact of our physical existence here on Earth. But there may be other dimensions existing that are higher than our own. From our perspective here in the three-dimensional world, what might we understand about them? Some theoretical physicists today conceive of ten-dimensions as the reality of our universe. While a ten-dimensional universe can be formulated mathematically, visualizing and understanding such a place (places really) is essentially impossible within our three-dimensional perspective. Does this mean that such things cannot exist?

There are a couple of interesting references that can help us to better appreciate dimensionality. The first is a relatively old book, published in 1884, by Edwin Abbott entitled "Flatland-A Romance of Many Dimensions" (62). In his book, Abbott described the lifestyle of two-dimensional people who inhabit the imaginary two-dimensional world of Flatland. Interestingly, Abbott was neither a scientist nor a mathematician, but rather a school headmaster whose field was the classics. He conjured up a whole two-dimensional society with their own quirks and rules of behavior. Women were straight lines. Soldiers and the lowest classes of workmen were triangles. Middle class Flatlanders were equilateral triangles. Professional men and gentlemen were squares or pentagons. Members of the nobility were hexagons, rising up to polygons. And finally, the priests were circles.

Abbott indicated some of the physical constraints that would be encountered in a two-dimensional universe. For a person living in Flatland, the visual appearance of all objects (except women end-on) would be as straight lines, even though they would actually be two dimensional plane figures such as triangles, squares, polygons, and circles. For example, a large circle would appear as a long line, while a small circle would appear as a short line. Two-dimensional objects that might be present inside the outer objects would not visible to the Flatland observer. Thus, the "internal organs" of Flatland inhabitants could not be seen. Nor could the insides of the Flatland dwellings, which by the way were universally pentagonal in shape. A line feature would present an absolute physical barrier to a Flatlander. He could only circumvent it by going around it peripherally. Gaining entrance to a pentagonal home in Flatland could only be had by passing through open line segments on the faces of the pentagon.

The concepts of Abbott about Flatland have been significantly extended to out-of-body and near-death experiences in an article published by Brumblay (63).

Brumblay considered what a two-dimensional being might experience if he were suddenly thrust into a three-dimensional environment. Basically, the Flatlander is elevated and floating above his two-dimensional landscape. When this happens, all of the two-dimensional constraints will be immediately removed. The Flatlander will be able to see through his two-dimensional line barriers. He will have a 360 degree view of his two-dimensional environment, and will be able to see the shapes of the triangles, squares, polygons, and circles that he previously could only see in the form of line segments. He will also be able to see any features that may be present inside these two-dimensional figures.

Now he can see through what to him were previously "walls", and look inside Flatlander houses. He could see the Flatlanders in their true forms, and also to see their "internal organs". Naturally, this would be very disconcerting to him, since he would still possess his two-dimension way of thinking and discerning.

In moving from two-dimensions to three-dimensions, the extracted Flatlander would become invisible to the inhabitants of Flatland because he now existed in the third-dimension, which is completely inaccessible to them.

The extracted Flatlander would also have the ability to predict future experiences of his fellow Flatlanders to some degree. To see this, consider a Flatlander who is moving through a two-dimensional maze. The extracted Flatlander would be able to know in advance what future events the maze Flatlander would encounter based on the choices that were made while traversing the maze. He would know what the future event-options were for the maze traversal.

In his new three-dimensional environment, the extracted Flatlander would have freedom of movement in three dimensions, rather than just two. He could essentially traverse his previous line "walls" by simply hopping over them. He could translate and rotate his three-dimensional "astral body". The extracted Flatlander would be aware of a three-dimensional environment that was totally foreign to him and his two-dimensional way of thinking. He would be forced to learn and adapt to his new higher dimensional universe.

Given this background as to what could be expected in moving from two-to three-dimensions, the next logical step is to extrapolate as to what might be expected in moving from three-to four-dimensions.

In our three dimensional world, we know of left-right, up-down, and forward-backward. But we have no concept at all of the nature of a fourth spatial dimension, which I will, for lack of a better terminology, call "in-out". What the dickens might "in-out" be? We haven't the slightest idea until we can actually experience it. Abbott devoted a significant section of Flatland to attempts by a three-dimensional being to describe the third dimension to a two-dimensional being, with absolutely no success.

So what might a three-dimensional person who somehow finds himself in a four-dimensional "astral body" experience? Here are some speculations, based on the two-to three-dimensional scenario.

First, he would be invisible to three-dimensional observers. He would be able to see through walls and see the interior features of closed, three-dimensional objects—he could see the internal organs of his fellow three-dimensional humans. It is possible that he might have a completely spherical field of view, that is, he would be able to see in all of the spherical directions simultaneously. Time as we know it in the three-dimensional world might be different, perhaps even non-existent, in a four-dimensional world. It might be possible to view past, present, and future simultaneously. Just as with the two-dimensional being in three-dimensions, there would be a very significant dislocation in perception of the higher dimensional reality. Our fourth-dimensional voyager would be quite confused and apprehensive until he obtained at least a little familiarity with his new surroundings. It would take him a while to modify his three-dimensional view of the four-dimensional world.

Another way to contemplate a non-physical reality is through thinking about the reality experienced by a photon of light (or any other wavelength in the electromagnetic spectrum). Light has significant non-physical aspects. As we have shown, a photon of light possesses no mass and no charge (although it does possess a "spin" whatever that is). Furthermore, from our perspective a photon must always be in motion, moving at the speed of light from the point where it is generated to the point where it is absorbed by matter. There is no such thing as a stationary photon in our physical worldview.

Let's ask ourselves the question: What is it like to be a photon? This is a takeoff on the famous question "what is it like to be a bat" that was raised by one of the consciousness researchers in order to probe the nature of consciousness qualia.

First of all a photon is a fundamental "bit" or quantum of electromagnetic radiation. The light beam from a laser is formed from a vast assembly of photons, all with the particular wavelength of the laser radiation, that move at the speed of light from their point of generation at the laser to the point where they run into something that either absorbs, reflects, or scatters them.

Electromagnetic radiation is described as a periodically varying electric field in one plane and a periodically varying magnetic field in a perpendicular plane, with the direction of motion of the radiation the direction represented by the intersection of both planes. The local electric and magnetic fields in the photon are considered to be "what is waving".

The electromagnetic spectrum of radiation is characterized by the wavelength and frequency of the radiation. These two are related in that the frequency of the radiation is the reciprocal of the wavelength (the speed of light being in both formulations). The electromagnetic spectrum is considered by physicists to be "open ended", in that both very long wavelengths and very short wavelengths are possible. At the current time, the longest wavelengths observed are in the range of 100,000,000 meters (extremely low frequency radiation), while the shortest wavelengths are in the range of 0.0000000000001 meters (gamma rays). In principal, the limiting long wavelength is the diameter of the universe, and the limiting short wavelength is the Planck length which is an unimaginably small 0.0000000000000000000000000000000001 meter. The wavelengths we can see with our physical eyes are in the range of 0.000000390-0.000000750 meters.

You may ask yourself, well if the photon is a little packet of electromagnetic radiation, what is the size and shape of the photon? The answer is that physicists do not have a good answer to this question. Depending on observation, the photon can behave either as a particle or a wave. If it is particle-like, then physicists will tell you that it has no size or shape; it is fundamentally just an ideal point. If it is wave-like, then the basic size of the photon may be related to its wavelength, but only in some nebulous way.

Adopting the "worldview" of the photon, one can say that the photon exists outside of spacetime as we know it. This is because Einstein's theory of relativity says that for a particle moving near the speed of light, the particle length gets shorter and its local time gets slower with respect to an observer who is not moving relative to the particle. Now photons always move at the speed of light so, for the photon, there is no time and no distance or movement. From the photon's perspective, it is a stationary entity in the "void". It comes into existence at a "place" and goes out of its existence at the same "place".

So what is it like to be a photon? It is very different indeed from what it is like to be a human being living in the physical reality we perceive with our senses. It is basically outside our spacetime reality.

The previous discussion was designed to give you a feeling for the non-physical nature of Universal Consciousness. What do we really know as physical human beings about its non-physical nature? One thing we may be able to say based upon quantum mechanical observations is that this non-physical nature is most probably nonlocal in the sense that interactions can take place instantaneously or at least much, much, much faster than the speed limit of light in the physical reality. Because Universal Consciousness is nonlocal, this may imply that everything in that overarching reality is interconnected in a very intimate way. Another thing we can say is that Physical

Reality is but a subset of an all-encompassing Universal Consciousness Reality.

If our perception of Physical Reality is a subset of a larger Universal Consciousness Reality, then it is the source of everything in the Physical Reality that possesses the fundamental of consciousness. The question then becomes how far down consciousness goes in the hierarchy of physical entities.

It is clear that we human beings possess the fundamental of consciousness. The one thing we know for certain is that we are conscious beings who realize their own existence. If we ever make contact with intelligent entities not of this Earth (a highly likely prospect given the explosion in the number of planets that continue to be discovered orbiting distant stars), they too will certainly possess consciousness.

But what about the vast number of other living species here on Earth (and perhaps elsewhere in the universe)? My intuitive feeling is that every living thing possesses some level of consciousness. Consciousness is the key ingredient for life. This of course begs the question: What is life? The encyclopedic definition of life typically goes something like this (64):

> *Animate beings share a range of properties and phenomena that are not seen together in inanimate matter, although examples of matter exhibiting one or the other of these can be found. Living entities metabolize, grow, die, reproduce, respond, move, have*

> *complex organized functional structures, heritable variability, and have lineages which can evolve over generational time, producing new and emergent functional structures that provide increased adaptive fitness in changing environments. Reproduction involves not only the replication of the nucleic acids that carry the genetic information but the epigenetic building of the organism through a sequence of developmental steps. Such reproduction through development occurs within a larger life-cycle of the organism, which includes its senescence and death. Something that is alive has organized, complex structures that carry out these functions as well as sensing and responding to interior states and to the external environment and engaging in movement within that environment.*

I feel that if something can die, then it possesses at least some level of consciousness within it. This applies to species like dolphins, whales, elephants, chimpanzees, apes, dogs and cats, and all other animals that seem to have at least a rudimentary self-awareness. But my intuition further tells me that it goes all the way down the ladder of living things. It includes all animals, insects, plants, and even down to life forms as lowly as amoeba and bacteria.

Although all living things possess consciousness, it is clear that the level of that consciousness varies vastly. The consciousness level of a dog is clearly significantly lower than that of a human being; the consciousness of an ant is orders of magnitude below that of a dog; and the consciousness of a bacterium is orders of magnitude below that of an ant.

If one is going to say that bacteria possess consciousness, then it begs the question: Do each of the cells in our body have an individual consciousness? Are our blood cells and skin cells and brain cells individually conscious at some extremely low level? If so, then how do these cellular consciousnesses relate to the overall consciousness of the human being? Is human consciousness the sum total of the individual cellular consciousnesses, or is the human consciousness something distinct from what you might call the "body consciousness"? I wish I knew.

Along these lines of thought, one particular type of human cell stands out, the HeLa cell. HeLa cells are cancer cells that were taken from the body of Henrietta Lacks before she died of cancer in 1951. They are called HeLa based on a shortened form of her first and last name, and are a major strain of cells used for biomedical cancer research. HeLa cells are regarded as "immortal" because, unlike other cells in the body that have a limited lifetime, these cells can divide an unlimited number of times under the proper culturing conditions. The number of HeLa cells grown since 1951 when Henrietta Lacks died far exceeds the total number of cells that were originally in her alive body. Now these HeLa cells are clearly no longer associated with Henrietta Lacks although they were originally from her. They have an independent existence of their own. So do they also possess a rudimentary consciousness?

After bacteria, things get even more fuzzy. What about viruses? Viruses are usually described as "semi-life". They reproduce their genetic DNA or RNA chemical makeup, but they cannot do so on their own. They need to invade a living cell in order to reproduce. Do viruses "die"? Viruses would appear to be the transition from living things to non-living things. They possess aspects of both living bacteria and non-living molecules.

A key question to ask is whether non-living things possess any level of consciousness at all. There are those who say the answer to this is yes. In his book "From Science to God", Peter Russell puts forth the premise that everything physical, even inanimate objects, possess some level of consciousness, even if it is almost vanishingly small (65). This would include things like crystals, metals, beach sand, water, and even the air you breathe. At the lowest level, it would go from molecules, chemicals, elements, atoms, and all the way down to basic atomic particles such as protons, neutrons, and electrons, and even to the even more basic subatomic particles. At the higher levels, it would mean that dirt, rocks, rivers, the ocean, and even the planet Earth possess a consciousness (there are some who call the Earth consciousness Gaia). And at the highest levels, it would include stars, galaxies, and ultimately the entire physical universe.

Another person who has put forward a non-physical theory of the physical is Rupert Sheldrake in his book "A New Science of Life: The Hypothesis of Formative Causation" (66). Sheldrake's book caused quite a violent reaction in the scientific community when it was first published. The editor at the time of the distinguished scientific journal Nature stated the following in a published editorial:

*Even bad books should not be burned; works
such as Mein Kampf have become historical
documents for those concerned with the
pathology of politics. But what is to be made
of Dr. Rupert Sheldrake's book "A New Science
of Life"? This infuriating tract has been widely
hailed by newspapers and popular science
magazines as the "answer" to materialistic
science . . . .*

*The author, by training a biochemist and
by demonstration a knowledgeable man,
is however, misguided. His book is the best
candidate for burning there has been for many
years.*

This was certainly a furious attack by the editor of Nature.
This editor died in 2009 and that brings to mind the quote
from the famous physicist Max Planck in association
with his own paradigm-shifting discovery of the energy
quantum: *A new scientific truth does not triumph by
convincing its opponents and making them see the light, but
rather because its opponents eventually die.*

Sheldrake's hypothesis of formative causation puts forth
the idea that "morphogenetic fields" and "morphic
resonance" in these fields are responsible for the
development of the forms that natural systems take, at
all levels of complexity from the molecular to the human
being. He has posited that these morphogenetic fields and
resonances are non-physical in nature, having no mass or
energy but simply conveying information about "form"
in some undetermined way. Given this, he also assumed

DR. JOHN J. PETROVIC

that these effects were not attenuated by time and space, in essence that they lay outside of spacetime.

What is the source of the morphogenetic fields and resonances? Here is what Sheldrake had to say (66):

> But then what determines the particular form of the morphogenetic field? One possible answer is that morphogenetic fields are eternal. They are simply given, and not explicable in terms of anything else. Thus even before this planet appeared, there already existed in a latent state the morphogenetic fields of all the chemicals, crystals, animals, and plants that have ever occurred on Earth, or that will ever come into being in the future . . .
>
> The other possible answer is radically different. Chemical and biological forms are repeated not because they are determined by changeless laws or eternal forms, but because of a causal influence from previous similar forms. This influence would require an action across space and time unlike any known type of physical action . . . In this case, what determines the form on the first occasion? No scientific answer can be given: the question concerns unique and energetically indeterminate events . . .
>
> This new way of thinking is unfamiliar, and it leads into uncharted territory. But only by exploring it does there seem to be any hope of arriving at a new scientific understanding of

form and organization in general, and of living
organisms in particular.

One can see that what Sheldrake proposed was a lot to swallow by the physical reality scientific establishment in 1981 and the same applies today, but it does seem to have some elements in common with the idea of Universal Consciousness.

Sheldrake's ideas apply to both living and non-living things and he has provided some thought-provoking evidence in support of them. With regard to non-living things, Sheldrake presented observations that the melting points of new chemical compounds tend to increase with time from the time they are first discovered. He cited a comparison of changes with time in the melting points of naturally occurring salicin and synthetic acetylsalicylic acid (commonly known as aspirin) with time as measured at various dates in the twentieth century. The melting point of salicin is unchanged throughout the entire twentieth century and Sheldrake attributes this melting point stability to the fact that salicin has been naturally occurring for millions of years and thus its "form" associated with its morphogenetic fields has been in place and is now static. On the other hand, acetylsalicylic acid (aspirin) was first chemically synthesized in 1853 and introduced into medical usage in 1899. He showed data indicating that the melting point of aspirin increased by 8 degrees centigrade from the beginning to the end of the twentieth century, and he attributed this melting point rise to the refinement of its "form" with time under the action of the morphogenetic fields. Conventional chemists argue that this increase in melting point is due to increasing purity of a new compound with time. However Sheldrake claims that they can provide no solid evidence that establishes such increasing purity with time.

So where do I stand on the question of how pervasive consciousness is in the physical reality? My intuition strongly tells me that every living thing contains the fundamental of consciousness, with the amount of that consciousness increasing as the level of complexity of the living thing increases. The consciousness levels of a human being and an amoeba are vastly different. But on the question whether non-living things possess consciousness, my intuition is ambivalent. It would make a nice, all-encompassing view of Universal Consciousness if consciousness went all the way down to the subatomic particle level, as suggested by Russell and Sheldrake, but I find a certain reluctance within myself to take that additional intuitive leap. My intuitive inclination is that all non-living things, from subatomic particles to celestial bodies, can be created, manipulated by, and are contained within the Universal Consciousness, but that they lack its essence. I cannot bring myself to embrace the concept that the air I breathe, the water I drink, the rock on the ground, and the other inanimate objects that I encounter every day contain any amount of consciousness. However, I have to say that this is only my uncertain intuitive feeling; I could very well be wrong.

Now let's proceed to a discussion of some of the characteristics that are most likely possessed by the Universal Consciousness. The first and most important aspect is that the Universal Consciousness is non-physical. It exists in some way outside of our physical spacetime reality, yet it is the source of our consciousness and of all the physical things that surround us. We can only begin to understand this non-physicality using analogies, so let us try by using the phenomena of dark matter, dark energy, and black holes in this vein.

Dark matter and dark energy are presently considered by science to comprise 96% of our physical reality universe. All the matter and energy that we can detect with our latest scientific instruments accounts for only 4% of the known physical universe.

In the late 1960's, astronomers discovered that the stars located at the outer edges of galaxies were moving faster than would be expected based on the visible amount of mass near the center of these galaxies. This observation led to the conclusion that all the galaxies in the observable universe are encased inside spherical globes of what they called dark matter. It was termed "dark" because this new type of matter does not emit or scatter light or any other form of electromagnetic radiation. Scientific observations suggest that this dark matter is not formed of atoms and their proton, neutron, and electron constituents, but rather some unknown form of matter that does not interact with ordinary physical matter in any way except through gravitational effects. One way to think about this is that a tremendous number of dark matter particles stream through your body every second of your lifetime, but do not interact with your body at all so that you never feel them or know that they are passing through you. Scientists have been trying to find explanations for dark matter in the decades since it was discovered but have thus far been unsuccessful. Dark matter is presently something that can clearly be classified as outside the realm of our conventional science.

Then there is the even more mysterious dark energy. In 1998, astronomers studying the spectral characteristics of a certain type of supernova called a type 1a supernova as a function of the supernova's distance from Earth discovered a totally unexpected result. Their data showed that the rate of expansion of the universe was accelerating, rather than decelerating as expected from cosmological theories up to that time. What this meant is that empty space was exerting a negative pressure on itself, resulting in an acceleration. One can think of this phenomenon something like this. Consider a cube of totally empty space. Now, even though this cube of empty space has nothing in it, it will exert a negative pressure on the empty space that is surrounding it, thus causing the space to expand and accelerate away from itself. It's as if there was "something" inside empty space that was producing a negative gravitational field. This "something" cosmologists have called "dark energy", not for any good reason but simply to put a label on the phenomenon. In fact, our current science has absolutely no idea as to what dark energy might be. So at the moment dark energy, like dark matter, is outside the realm of our conventional science, way outside the realm.

The final analogy I would like to discuss in association with the non-physical aspects of Universal Consciousness is the singularity at the center of a cosmological black hole. A black hole is a region of spacetime whose gravity is so intense that not even light can escape from it (hence the reason that it is called "black"). Black holes form when a star explodes in a supernova. There are thought to be many black holes wandering around the universe, and our Milky Way galaxy has a supermassive black hole at its center. Each black hole has what is called an "event horizon" which surrounds it. If matter or energy passes through this event horizon, then it can never escape. Rather, this entrapped matter and energy swirls down and down until it reaches the black hole center. What is at the center of a black hole? Our science does not really know. Current theories predict there is a "gravitational singularity" at the black hole center where the curvature of spacetime becomes infinite and the laws of physics as we know them break down completely. Some theorists think that spacetime may become "quantum granular" at the black hole center, because the center will be almost infinitely small yet almost infinitely dense. Others think that a rift in spacetime may occur at the center, crossing dimensions and spewing out matter and energy somewhere else in the universe at a "white hole". The center of a black hole is indeed a place beyond the realm of our conventional science.

Hopefully, the above discussion will help you to have at least of feel for the concept of Universal Consciousness being non-physical in comparison to what we understand physical reality to be. Now one must ask: How does Universal Consciousness influence our physical reality? What does it do? My intuition tells me that one important thing Universal Consciousness does is to transmit awareness. Universal Consciousness is the source of awareness for all entities who are aware, even at the most rudimentary levels. At the higher levels of consciousness (such as ourselves) this information can be interpreted as "thought". Perhaps we can "think" of Universal Consciousness as an "awareness field". There is no speed limit for the transmission of awareness and thought through the Universal Consciousness "field". Transmission of such things is absolutely instantaneous. In other words, it is "spooky action at a distance", something that has been actually observed in quantum mechanical experiments on the borderline of our physical reality. The speed of awareness and thought is instantaneous. My intuition is that Universal Consciousness can create entities with awareness simply through the transmission of the thought of awareness.

In addition, Universal Consciousness has the ability to create matter and energy out of nothing more than "pure thought". Now, my intuitive view is that inanimate non-living matter and energy are not conscious and hence are not created by the transmission of awareness. Rather, these inanimate objects are created by bringing them into physical existence through the thought action of the Universal Consciousness. How can this be? Again, it is only possible to fall back to physical reality analogies and that is what we will do.

So let's talk about "zero point energy". You might think that there was nothing in a vacuum. But physicists will tell you quantum mechanical theory predicts that the empty space of a vacuum is actually filled with a tremendous quantity of "virtual" radiation and particles. The term "virtual" here means they do not exist in our physical reality until they somehow mysteriously "pop" into physical existence. So there is thought to be a stupendous amount of "something" in what we perceive as "nothing". The zero point energy is the energy of all the "fields" that exist in the vacuum because the absolute ground state energy of a photon or particle is not zero but rather has a value of ½ hν. One can think of this energy as the sum total of a vast number of virtual photons that exist in the vacuum. These virtual photons range over the entire known electromagnetic spectrum, from the longest wavelengths to the very shortest wavelengths (taken to be the Planck length of the order of 10^{-35} meters, which is smaller than a proton by about a billion billion times).

Now you might think this is nonsense, but there are actually experimental results suggesting that the zero point energy really exists. These experiments involve the so-called Casimir Effect. If you take two parallel plates of a material and move them extremely close to each other, the plates will experience an attractive force between them. The reason for this attractive force is that as the plates get extremely close together, some of the zero point wavelengths will be excluded from the gap between the plates because the gap is smaller than these wavelengths. So effectively, the zero point energy exerts a pressure on the plates tending to push them together. This zero point pressure only becomes significant for very small plate spacings. For example, at a plate spacing of 0.000000001 meter, the Casimir pressure on the plates is one atmosphere (14.7 pounds per square inch), and it becomes vanishingly small as the plate spacing increases.

Having tried our best to describe what the Universal Consciousness might be like, we now reduce our focus to a much more local level. We ask ourselves how does the "I", our own consciousness, relate to the Universal Consciousness?

Some people believe that the "I" constitutes the entirety of Universal Consciousness. However, my intuitive feeling is that our "I" is just a very miniscule bit of the Universal Consciousness. One can think about this using the analogy of a drop of rain water in comparison to the vast ocean. Both the single drop of rain water and the vast ocean are made of the same molecular essence, H_2O. They are essentially the same in their fundamental chemical formula. But the drop of rain water is isolated from the ocean until the time that it falls back into the ocean and loses its individuality. Furthermore, the ocean has a vastly greater power and influence than does a single drop of water. What happens in the ocean affects the entire Earth; however, the same cannot be said for a single rain drop.

As we discussed previously, you cannot really locate the "I", you can only feel its presence as the aspect of awareness. If you look deeply inside yourself, you will feel that the "I" is there, observing and experiencing the events of your life. You come closest to experiencing the "I" during those times of deep meditation. These are the times when you have no thoughts in your mind, only the presence of your existence. At these times, only the "I" is present, the little bit of Universal Consciousness that is the true you. In the spiritual sense, one might say the "I" is your soul.

If the "I" is your soul, then what is your mind? And how does your mind relate to the soul as well as the brain? The neuroimaging results of Beauregard on the placebo effect indicate that subjective feelings and expectations have a significant influence on various levels of brain functioning at the molecular, cellular, and neural levels (13). So it would appear that "mind" is much more than just materialistic brain functioning. Beauregard put forward the following "Psychoneural Translation Hypothesis" to explain his neuroimaging results (13):

> To interpret these results of all the neuroimaging studies reviewed in this article, we need a hypothesis that accounts for the relationship between mental activity and brain activity. The Psychoneural Translation Hypothesis (or PTH) is such a hypothesis. It posits that the mind (the psychological world, the first-person perspective) and the brain (which is part of the "physical" world, the third-person perspective) represent two epistemologically and ontologically distinct domains that can interact because they are complementary aspects of the same underlying reality. According to the PTH, mind (including consciousness) represents an irreducible and fundamental aspect of our world. Furthermore, the PTH postulates that conscious and unconscious mental processes/events, which are neurally grounded, are selectively translated, based on a specific code, into neural processes/events at the various levels of brain organization (biophysical, molecular, chemical, neural circuits). In turn, the resulting neural processes/events are translated into processes and events in other physiological systems, such as the immune or endocrine system (the communication between the mind, the brain, and the other physiological systems constitute a psychosomatic network) . . . . . Metaphorically, we could say that mentalese

> *(the language of the mind) is translated into neuronese (the language of the brain).*

The quantum physicist Henry Stapp has developed quantum mechanical formalisms to argue that the mind is something distinct from the brain, adopting the quantum mechanical formalism of John von Neumann (67). Von Neumann's reasoning was that consciousness was the only observer that could be outside the expanded quantum mechanical system to cause the collapse of the wave function from an infinity of possibilities to the one actually observed. Thus to von Neumann, consciousness created reality. While the physical brain can be incorporated as part of the quantum mechanical system, the consciousness, the mind, cannot because it is something that is not physical in nature.

We certainly know that we have a conscious mind. When we wake up each morning, we are in the conscious state. During that time, we take inputs from our five senses, and we have coherent thought processes. However, each night when we go to sleep, we pass from the conscious state to the unconscious state. I have attempted to assess my own transition from consciousness to unconsciousness in approaching the sleep state. I am definitely conscious and concentrating on remaining conscious up to a certain point. But then a veil seems to come down relatively rapidly and I am unconscious and in the state of sleep. I do not seem able to modify this transition with the concentration of my conscious mind. The transition from consciousness to unconsciousness during sleep is a rapid one once it begins.

Additionally, we can be made to go abruptly from the waking conscious state to the unconscious state artificially through the use of anesthetics. There is also the physical trauma aspect of consciousness. If someone hits you on the head hard enough, you will immediately transition from the conscious to the unconscious state. Finally, drugs can affect the brain to cause a state of unconsciousness. Abnormal brain chemistry can also produce mental illnesses of the conscious state such as depression and schizophrenia which can be relieved by the administration of appropriate drugs.

The above observations make it patently evident that waking consciousness is associated with brain function in significant measure. However, people have been trying for years to determine where in the brain consciousness is located. All the research that has been done thus far indicates that consciousness is a generalized brain function that draws from many different physical locations in the brain.

But the question is: Do we also have another level of mind that is distinct from our conscious mind? I refer of course to the subconscious mind. Sigmund Freud thought we did. He felt that the subconscious mind (he called it the unconscious mind) was the storehouse of repressed memories and desires. Freud's analogy of the mind was an iceberg. The conscious mind was that part above the water, while the subconscious was below the water line. As with an iceberg, the subconscious was significantly larger than the conscious, and was the site of a great many negative things such as fears, violent motives, unacceptable sexual desires, immoral urges, irrational wishes, selfish needs, and shameful experiences.

While I agree with Freud that we have a subconscious mind, I believe that it is positive in nature and much more encompassing than what Freud conceived it to be. In contrast to Freud's iceberg floating in water, the analogy of an ocean liner is a good one for expressing my view on the subconscious. Part of the ocean liner is under water, but the bulk of the ship is above water. The part of the ship below the waterline can be taken as our conscious mind, while the larger portion of the ship represents our subconscious. The two parts of the ship are connected to each other but the environments they experience are distinctly different. The below-water part sees only the dimly lit water immediately around it, while the above-water part experiences a great expanse of sea and sky. Furthermore, the above-water part can see where the ship is headed, while this is invisible to the below-water. Using this analogy, the subconscious mind is much larger in scope than the conscious mind, and has greatly expanded abilities and perceptions that are not present in the conscious mind.

What is the evidence that we have an expansive subconscious mind? First consider hypnosis, a state that appears to allow some level of direct access to the subconscious. Under hypnosis, people can remember details of events that they cannot remember in the conscious state. Indeed, hypnosis has been used in criminal investigations to help reveal details of events from witnesses that they simply cannot recall when they are consciously aware. People also recall childhood memories from long ago in vivid detail. These memories reside in the subconscious mind.

Under hypnosis, people can be made to exhibit physical reactions that would be very difficult under the control of their conscious mind. If it is suggested that they will feel no pain when pricked with a pin, they will not feel pain. If a suggestion is made of some painful trauma, then they will experience that pain even though no trauma has occurred. Through post-hypnotic suggestions, people can be made to perform actions while in the conscious state that they have not conceived in their conscious mind. These things are possible because hypnosis is somehow able to gain access to and influence the subconscious mind.

Another manifestation of the subconscious mind occurs in the dreams we have during REM sleep. We are not conscious, but our mind is functioning in a semi-coherent way. We can "experience" many things in our dreams, some bizarre and some relatively mundane. People often have recurrent dreams. Some dreams combine conscious memories with subconscious scenarios. Finally, unless we write them down immediately upon awakening, we rapidly forget most of our dreams.

But what happens to our mind during non-REM sleep? We have no level of consciousness then, not even a dream consciousness. Where am "I" during non-REM sleep? As far as I can tell, no one really knows. The scientific studies of non-REM sleep are rare indeed. This is because there are no rapid eye movements and no dreams to investigate. Yet brain waves are still being generated. My feeling is that "I" am ensconced in my subconscious mind during the periods of non-REM sleep. Non-REM sleep-like conditions can also be produced during deep meditative states. The "I" is there, but not the conscious. Only the subconscious.

How does one explain the mental feats that can be performed by savants? How does a savant calculate the value of pi, the ratio of the circumference of a circle to its diameter, out to twenty-five thousand decimal places in his head? How does another savant read and remember every name and telephone number in the New York City phone book? Or instantly recall everything that he has ever read in his life? Such mental feats are only possible through the use of the subconscious mind. They are not within the capacity of the conscious mind.

I believe that all creative thoughts originate in the subconscious mind. In the entire course of my 40-plus year scientific career, I have had a goodly number of interesting and useful ideas, many of which were translated into scientific journal publications. But I have only had four scientific ideas I would consider to be truly creative in nature, that constituted something entirely new. In each of these four cases, the kernel of the creative idea did not occur by any conscious, logical process. It simply "popped" into my awareness as a completely formed thought from somewhere other than my conscious mind. I think that "somewhere" was my subconscious mind.

So it is clear that we have a conscious mind and it is highly likely that we have an expansive subconscious mind. Where can we go from there? I believe we can proceed by viewing conscious and subconscious as manifestations of the Body-Mind-Soul interaction. Although it involves three parts, this view is fundamentally different from Freud's materialistic Id-Ego-SuperEgo mind formalism.

The interaction of the Body, in this case the brain, with the Mind is what constitutes the conscious part of Mind. This view accounts for all of the physical aspects of the transition from consciousness to unconsciousness, since these (sleep, anesthetics, physical trauma) all have an influence on the Body (brain) aspect of the Body-Mind interaction.

The subconscious mind comes from the Mind-Soul interaction. The Soul is considered to exist in a state of superconsciousness. This superconsciousness derives from the fact that the Soul, the "I", is a little bit of the Universal Consciousness essence. It is probably not possible for the conscious mind to begin to comprehend the range and extent of superconsciousness. Superconsciousness is associated with the "All" and with the "I Am".

But the Mind-Soul interaction elicits the subconscious Mind, which can be accessed to a limited degree by the conscious Mind. As I have pointed out, interactions between the subconscious and the conscious occur during hypnotic, dream, and meditative states, and may also be responsible for truly creative thought.

One may view the Mind aspects of the brain using the analogy of a television set. The electronics of the TV set are analogous to the neuron networks in the brain.

But the information being presented by the TV set does not have its source in the TV electronics. The information is transmitted from somewhere remote to the TV set via antenna, cable, or satellite connections. That "somewhere else" is related to the "I", the soul, the superconscious. This is the fundamental reason why we will never find the source of consciousness through a reductionist study of brain function. It simply does not lie within brain function. The brain acts as a receiver of information from the superconscious "I" through the action of the subconscious. The brain also probably filters out higher-level information that we do not need for our functioning here in the physical reality. By changing channels on a TV set, the electronics allow you to access different groups of information that are being broadcast. The brain is a filter that only allows us access to that portion of larger reality information that we can deal with in the context of our physical reality.

We can think of the conscious Mind as the "me", the ego, and the subconscious Mind as the "I". The ego is the personality that we have in this physical existence. The ego is the sum total of the things you have experienced and the people you have interacted with in your physical life. But the "me" is not the same as the "I"; the "me" is a subset of the much larger "I". The Mind we have in the physical reality is a combination of both "me and I".

What happens to the Mind when a person dies? At death, the brain no longer functions and the Body piece of the Body-Mind-Soul interaction is gone. When this happens, the subconscious takes over as the conscious portion of Mind in the Mind-Soul interaction. So, at death, we have full-time access to our subconscious Mind. Basically, after death our subconscious Mind becomes the consciousness of our existence in the new level of reality to which we have just transitioned. We realize that the "me", the ego that has been formed by the physical life we have just lived, is only a small element of the "I".

After physical death of the body, we continue to exist and have consciousness in a much larger reality. You might say that we metamorphose into conscious energy entities, "beings of light", our pure form of existence as little bits of Universal Consciousness. We return to the place from which we came, our true Home.

One might ask the following question: Is the Universal Consciousness what religious people call Brahman or Yahweh or Allah or God? My answer to this question is: Why not? Why not indeed.

The Dream I Dream

My dream began the day I was born and still continues. The dream has many vignettes that bubble through my mind.

First conscious awareness at age three. Interactions with loving parents and single male sibling. Everything gloriously new. First summer, first Christmas, first television show, first bicycle, first kindergarten class. Remember a great many details about first home and wonderful experiences there. Extended family group then with family living on second floor, maternal grandparents on first floor, and aunt's family in second home on same lot. Dream is safe and warm.

Dream scenes race by. Family's move from inner city to suburbs and delight of fresh, green, open surroundings. Brother is companion and best friend. New home, new school, new friends. Exciting adventures of youth, baseball, boy scouts, bike riding around neighborhood. Distributing newspapers to neighbors at 5 am in dead of winter. One mile walk to bus stop each morning to attend high school. New and more intense things to learn. Mercury astronauts launched into space. Pressure to achieve starts to build. First date and kiss at junior prom. First in family to attend college and feel responsibility to do well. In class when Kennedy assassinated. College a blur of studying for tests with little time for much else. Dream takes on more complexity.

Graduate school working for Ph.D in science. Apollo 11 lands on moon. Freedom of young adulthood. Hike Grand Canyon with brother. New friends from all over the world. Meet future wife at graduate student party. Give first scientific presentation. Military commitment after graduation. Ph.D and stint in military.

Civilian again with job at scientific lab. Marriage and in-laws. One year of two-ness, then baby. See new daughter in hospital at age two hours. Family to provide for now. Happy family trips to many places. Experience both good and bad events. Dream scary at times.

Daughter grows up and leaves home. After years, sell home and move to work in big city as prelude to retirement. Retire and relocate with wife to beautiful, warm spot. Daughter gets married. Pursue compulsion to write books about spirituality and reality.

That's my dream thus far.

But when my time comes, then I expect to truly wake up.

References

1. "The Mystery of the Mind", A Critical Study of Consciousness and the Human Brain, Wilder Penfield, Princeton University Press, Princeton, New Jersey, c. 1975.
2. "My Stroke of Insight", A Brain Scientist's Personal Journey, Jill Bolte Taylor, Viking Adult Publisher, c. 2006.
3. B. Libet, E.W. Wright, B. Feinstein, and D.K. Pearl, "Subjective Referral of the Timing for a Conscious Sensory Experience", Brain, vol. 102, 193-224 (1979).
4. B. Libet, C.A. Gleason, E.W. Wright, and D.K. Pearl, "Time of Conscious Intention to Act in Relation to Onset of Cerebral Activity (Readiness-Potential)", Brain, vol. 106, 623-642 (1983).
5. I. Fried, R. Mukamel, and G. Kreiman, "Internally Generated Preactivation of Single Neurons in Human Medial Frontal Cortex Predicts Volition", Neuron, vol. 69, 548-562 (2011).
6. "LSD—My Problem Child", Albert Hofmann, McGraw-Hill Book Company, New York, c. 1980.

7. H.B. Linton and R.J. Langs, "Subjective Reactions to Lysergic Acid Diethylamide (LSD-25)", Arch. Gen. Psychiatry, vol. 6, 352-368 (1962).

8. Peter Hannes, "LSD: Revelation of the Mind—Chapter 2", http://www.lsdexperience.com/frameset_chapter02.htm.

9. "The Nobel Prizes 1994", John F. Nash, Nobel Prize autobiography, Nobel Foundation, Stockholm, c. 1995.

10. M.A. Persinger and F. Healey, "Experimental Facilitation of the Sensed Presence: Possible Intercalation between the Hemispheres Induced by Complex Magnetic Fields", Journal of Nervous and Mental Disease, vol. 190, 533-541 (2002).

11. M.A. Persinger, K.S. Saroka, S.A. Koren, and L.S. St-Pierre, "The Electromagnetic Induction of Mystical and Altered States within the Laboratory", Journal of Consciousness Exploration & Research, vol. 1, 808-830 (2010).

12. H.K. Beecher, "The Powerful Placebo", Journal of the American Medical Association (JAMA), vol. 159, 1602-1606 (1955).

13. M. Beauregard, "Mind does really matter: Evidence from neuroimaging studies of emotional self-regulation, psychotherapy, and placebo effect", Progress in Neurobiology, vol. 81, 218-236 (2007).

14. "Lucid Dreaming", Robert Waggoner, Moment Point Press, Needham, Massachusetts, c. 2009.

15. M. Massimini, et.al., "Breakdown of Cortical Effective Connectivity During Sleep", Science, vol. 309, 2228-2232 (2005).

16. T.A. Nielsen, "A review of mentation in REM and NREM sleep: "Covert" REM sleep as a possible

reconciliation of two opposing models", Behavioral and Brain Sciences, vol. 23, 793-1121 (2000).

17. C. Bassetti, et.al., "SPECT during sleepwalking", The Lancet, vol. 356, 484-485 (2000).

18. M.T. Alkire, A.G. Hudetz, and G. Tononi, "Consciousness and Anesthesia", Science, vol. 322, 876-880 (2008).

19. Stanford Hypnotic Susceptibility Scale—Form C, Andre M. Weitzenhoffer and Ernest R. Hilgard, Stanford University, 1962.

20. A.A. Fingelkurts, et.al., "Hypnosis Induces a Changed Composition of Brain Oscillations in EEG: A Case Study", Contemporary Hypnosis, vol. 24, 3-18 (2007).

21. P. Maquet, et.al., "Functional Neuroanatomy of Hypnotic State", Biological Psychiatry, vol. 45, 327-333 (1999).

22. M.E. Faymonville, M. Boly, and S. Laureys, "Functional neuroanatomy of the hypnotic state", Journal of Physiology—Paris, vol. 99, 463-469 (2006).

23. A.H.K. Wobst, "Hypnosis and Surgery: Past, Present, and Future", Anesthesia & Analgesia, vol. 104, 1199-1206 (2007).

24. D.R. Patterson and M.P. Jensen, "Hypnosis and Clinical Pain", Psychological Bulletin, vol. 129, 495-521 (2003).

25. S.W.G. Derbyshire, et.al., "Cerebral activation during hypnotically induced and imagined pain", NeuroImage, vol. 23, 392-401 (2004).

26. "Quantum Enigma", Bruce Rosenblum and Fred Kuttner, Oxford University Press, New York, c. 2006.

27. "The Trouble with Physics", Lee Smolin, Houghton Mifflin Company, New York, c. 2006.
28. "Wholeness and the Implicate Order", David Bohm, Routledge & Kegan Paul, New York, c. 1980.
29. "The Physical World as a Virtual Reality", Brian Whitworth, Centre for Discrete Mathematics and Theoretical Computer Science Research Report Series 316, Massey University, Albany, Auckland, New Zealand, December 2007.
30. "Life After Life", Raymond A. Moody Jr., Bantam Books, New York, c. 1975.
31. "Light and Death", Michael Sabom, M.D., Zondervan Publishing House, Grand Rapids, MI, c. 1998.
32. P. van Lommel, R. van Wees, V. Meyers, I. Elfferich, "Near-death experience in survivors of cardiac arrest: a prospective study in the Netherlands", The Lancet, vol. 358, 2039-2045 (2001).
33. R.H. Smit, "Corroboration of the Dentures Anecdote Involving Veridical Perception in a Near-Death Experience", Journal of Near-Death Studies, vol. 27. no. 1, 47-61 (2008).
34. E.W. Cook, B. Greyson, and I. Stevenson, "Do Any Near-Death Experiences Provide Evidence for the Survival of Human Personality After Death? Relevant Features and Illustrative Case Reports", Journal of Scientific Exploration, vol. 12, no. 3, 377-406 (1998).
35. C.T. Tart, "Psychophysiological Study of Out-of-the-Body Experiences in a Selected Subject", Journal of the American Society for Psychical Research, vol. 62, 3-27 (1968).
36. "The End of Materialism", Charles T. Tart, New Harbinger Publications and Noetic Books, Oakland, California, c. 2009.

37. C.T. Tart, "Second Psychophysiological Study of Out-of-the-Body Experiences in a Selected Subject", International Journal of Parapsychology, vol. 9, 251-258 (1967).

38. "Journeys Out of the Body", Robert A. Monroe, Doubleday, New York, c. 1971.

39. "Far Journeys", Robert A. Monroe, Broadway Books, New York, c. 1985.

40. "Ultimate Journey", Robert A. Monroe, Broadway Books, New York, c. 1994.

41. "On Life after Death", Elisabeth Kubler-Ross, Ten Speed Press, Berkeley, California, c. 1991.

42. I. Stevenson, "Six Modern Apparitional Experiences", Journal of Scientific Exploration, vol. 9, no. 3, 351-366 (1995).

43. W. Crookes, "Notes of an Enquiry into the Phenomena called Spiritual during the years 1870-1873", Quarterly Journal of Science, January 1st 1871.

44. "The Conscious Universe: The Scientific Truth of Psychic Phenomena", Dean Radin, Harper Collins, New York, c. 1997.

45. "An Autobiographical Memoir", Ingo Swann, http://www.biomindsuperpowers.com/Pages/2.html, 1996.

46. H.E. Puthoff, "CIA-Initiated Remote Viewing Program at Stanford Research Institute", Journal of Scientific Exploration, vol. 10, 63-76 (1996).

47. "Mind-Reach: Scientists Look at Psychic Abilities", Russell Targ and Harold E. Puthoff, Hampton Roads Publishing Company, Charlottesville, Virginia, c. 1977.

48. "The Ingo Swann 1973 Remote Viewing probe of the planet Jupiter", Ingo Swann, http://www.remoteviewed.com/remote_viewing_jupiter.htm, 1996.

49. R. Targ and H. Puthoff, "Information transmission under conditions of sensory screening", Nature, vol. 251, 602-607 (1974).

50. "My Story", Uri Geller, Praeger, New York, c. 1975.

51. "Uri: A Journal of the Mystery of Uri Geller", Andrija Puharich, Anchor Press/Doubleday, New York, c. 1975.

52. "Experiments with Uri Geller at the Stanford Research Institute (SRI), http://www.youtube.com/watch?v=1_2iPZiH5sk, Parts 1-4.

53. "The Metal-benders", John Hasted, Routledg & Kegan Paul, London, c. 1981.

54. "I = Awareness", A.J. Deikman, Journal of Consciousness Studies, vol. 3, no. 4, 350-356 (1996).

55. D.J. Chalmers, "The Puzzle of Conscious Experience", Scientific American, December 1995, 62-68.

56. "Conversations on Consciousness", Susan Blackmore, Oxford University Press, Oxford, c. 2006.

57. R.G. Jahn, et.al., "Correlations of Random Binary Sequences with Pre-Stated Operator Intention: A Review of a 12-Year Program", Journal of Scientific Exploration, vol. 11, no. 3, 345-367 (1997).

58. P. Bancel and R.D. Nelson, "The GCP Event Experiment: Design, Analytical Methods, Results", Journal of Scientific Exploration, vol. 22, no. 3, 309-333 (2008).

59. R.D. Nelson, "Coherent Consciousness and Reduced Randomness: Correlations on September 11, 2001", Journal of Scientific Exploration, vol. 16, no. 4, 549-570 (2002).

60. "What is Life? (with Mind and Matter and Autobiographical Sketches)", Erwin Schroedinger, Cambridge University Press, Cambridge, c. 1958.

61. R.G. Mays and S.B. Mays, "The Phenomenology of the Self-Conscious Mind", Journal of Near-Death Studies, vol. 27, no. 1, 5-45 (2008).
62. "Flatland-A Romance of Many Dimensions", Edwin A. Abbott, (first published in 1884 under the pseudonym "A. Square"), Dover Publications, New York, c. 1992.
63. R.J. Brumblay, "Hyperdimensional Perspectives in Out-of-Body and Near-Death Experiences", Journal of Near-Death Studies, vol. 21, 201-221 (2003).
64. Stanford Encyclopedia of Philosophy, Edward N. Zalta, Editor, The Metaphysics Lab, Center for the Study of Language and Information, Stanford University, Stanford, California.
65. "From Science to God", Peter Russell, New World Library, Novato, California, c. 2002.
66. "A New Science of Life: The Hypothesis of Formative Causation", Rupert Sheldrake, Blond and Briggs, London, c. 1981.
67. J.M. Schwartz, H.P. Stapp, and M. Beauregard, "Quantum physics in neuroscience and psychology: a neurophysical model of mind-brain interaction", Philosophical Transactions of the Royal Society B, (2004).